STRIPER TALES

A COLLECTION OF SURFCASTING STORIES

Enjoy bud!

D.J. MULLER

Cover Art by Mark Jolliffe
Edited by Dave Anderson

Printed and bound in Canada

ArtBookbindery.com

ISBN 978-0-615-35003-5

DEDICATION

This book is dedicated to my wife Anna, whom without her patience and understanding (letting me travel and be away so much), I would have no fuel for my fire.

To my daughter Hillary, always a sweet breath of fresh air.

To my father, one tough old German!

To Bobby Matthews, a long-time ace. Always neutral and willing to lend an ear or offer some sound advice…a good friend to many. He always told me he wanted a book with stories, so I want to dedicate part of this book to him and to his wife who passed recently.

To Laura Jolliffe, I dedicate a part of this book for being the winner a major battle and for allowing Mark to do what he loves.

To Jesus Christ, "Our Father which art in heaven, hallowed be thy name."

TABLE OF CONTENTS

PART I
NEW JERSEY

PART II
NEW YORK

PART III
RHODE ISLAND

ACKNOWLEDGEMENTS

As with any comprehensive attempt to gather information for a book, there are many hands that go into the collective effort. This book had *many* hands. I wish to acknowledge all the contributors for their sacrifice and for their enthusiasm in getting their stories to me. I know I must have been a pain at times. To you: Here are your stories, forever enshrined in an awesome menagerie of tales about our passion.

I want to acknowledge perhaps one of the best artists drawing striped bass today, maybe ever, my dear friend Mark Jolliffe. He is an exceptional artist, a great fisherman, and a super friend. He is also the source of prolonged periods of uncontrollable laughing… usually when fishing.

I want to acknowledge also the guys of Fish Eye, on the 'travel team,' a collection of serious hardcore surfcasters that understand what it takes to truly fish the high surf for the prince of the skinny water, the striper: Mike "Doc" DePietro, Murty "Flounder" Murtagh, Raymond, "Dilly Dock" Carlson (I don't even know his first name), Bill "Darter" Lellis, Tommy Koz, Honey, and Geoff Turner. Without these guys, fishing would still be good, but would certainly lack the depth of the other part of traveling and fishing, the forging of friendships and the irreplaceable experiences that can only be shared while living together on the road. With their friendship is also an irrevocable trust…that is rare these days.

I also want to acknowledge my good friends Dave and Greta Anderson, my family in Massachusetts, or, uh, Rhode Island. Thanks to Dave for all his help. It has been great working (and laughing) with you and I look forward to doing more projects (and catching more fish) together in the near future.

INTRODUCTION

Stories freeze special moments in time but if the stories are not told or recorded, time passage can steal them away and scatter their details into oblivion. If left for one to remember in his own head, one's fragile mind can become distorted, details forgotten and sizes of fish may grow to extraordinary lengths and weights. Maybe that is a good thing? I don't know, but this is also why it is so important to record and capture them.

I figure stories are a lot like pictures, they capture a special moment forever. Where a picture might say, "Oh yeah I remember that," it is the story behind it that gives it life. It gives it depth and color kind of like a picture in 3-D. A picture can't give you details about the way you felt or how hard it was to get to that point where the picture was taken. While a picture might offer a window back to a great moment, it's the story that lays out the drama, elicits the laughter, the tears, the satisfaction or the heartache—the story brings you into the picture to live inside the moment and feel what the teller felt, for a little while.

Photos are great reminders but it's the stories behind them that we really remember. So, I pass this collection of stories on to you, they will live long after we all graduate to the Big Surf.

* * *

I find it extremely humorous and ironic that in the collecting of the stories for this book I had a great degree of difficulty extracting them from perhaps the best storytellers of all-time...surf fishermen. Fishermen, the world around, are known as notorious "storytellers," I might venture to say even "liars" by those that know them best. Not once have I ever heard a group of surfcasters gather in a tackle shop and sit quietly, staring at each other and passively discussing politics or exchanging recipes for Yankee Pot Roast.

It is actually quite the opposite, these guys think out their stories and wild schemes, planning them with precision while listening to the "storyteller" across the counter finishing telling his tale. Those in attendance can't wait to spew the details of their latest adventure, with an audience on hand! Yet, in my efforts to extract a couple classics from this very same crowd, I might equate it to pulling a tooth with a pair of channel locks!

I often wonder how many great stories a surfman takes with him to the afterlife. How many unbelievable stories are swept away with the last breath of an expiring fisherman? I have traveled the northeast immersing myself in rocks, sand and salt water looking for our prince of the surf, the mighty striped bass. I have sat in infamous places: the front porch of the Cuttyhunk Fishing Club, Paulie's of Montauk, The Saltwater Edge in Rhode Island, Larry's Bait and Tackle on the Vineyard and I have listened, for years, to the yarns shared of adventures from both yesterday and yesteryear. In reflection I thought it necessary to enshrine some of those tales (the extractable ones) and to put them into a collection for all to read, a place where they truly belong!

I present to you a compilation of stories built around the striper and those that pursue them with vengeance and passion and for the love of the pull of the mighty bass against ones rod. I hope you enjoy the stories found here and perhaps one day your story too, can be recorded in the annals of striper fishing history.

A picture is only worth 1000 words after you have read them.
-DJ Muller

THE NON-SURFCASTERS GLOSSARY OF TERMS/SLANG

Belt/Waderbelt - Goes around the waist over your waders and drytop. It is used to keep water out of your waders should you fall in. Also used to carry tools, such as pliers, Boga Grip, and other things.

Blind Cast - Casting to quiet water for no obvious reason. A common practice.

Blitz - A time of heightened fish feeding activity when fish strike at almost anything making them very easy to catch.

Boga Grip - A tool used by surfcasters to control fish and to weigh them.

Bucktail - A type of lure. Has a leadhead and hair from a deer tail hence the name "bucktail."

Bunker - A slang name for one of the stripers favorite baitfish. It's real name: Atlantic menhaden, also called a pogy or mossbunker.

Drag - The mechanism built into a fishing reel that is used to slow down the run of a fish.

Dropper/Teaser - Small fish attractor that is attached ahead of the lure usually made of feather and hair (fly) and sometimes rubber; replicates a small baitfish.

Gaff - A large hook attached to a long wood or bamboo handle.

Gear up - Getting all of your gear and clothing on for a fishing excursion.

Googan - (a.k.a. a goog, newbie) A beginner, new to the sport.

Hit - The strike of a fish as it bites lure or bait.

Korkers - A commonly-used cleated rubber sole that is attached to the bottom of a surfcaster's boot to keep him from sliding on wet, slimy rocks.

Leader - A length of heavy monofilament that is attached to running line coming from reel.

Mono - Short for monofilament, a type of clear fishing line.

Pencil - A type of popper, lure that is fished across the surface of the water commonly grouped together as "topwater plugs".

Plug - Another name for a lure.

Plugbag - A bag commonly worm by a surfcaster to carry a plethora of plugs.

Point - An area of shoreline that sticks out into the water further than the rest of the shoreline. It could be comprised of sand or rock.

Rip - An area where two currents collide or where moving water is forced through a smaller space or over an underwater obstruction. All of these circumstances create turbulent water and fish congregate in these areas

Schoolie- A common term for a small striped bass.

Swell- A rolling body of water, usually associated with the early stage of a building wave.

Swimmer- A type of lure made of wood or plastic that wiggles when retrieved.

The Stranger

Who's the stranger
Mommie dear?
Look-he knows us!
Ain't he queer?

Hush my own-
don't talk so wild!
That's your father,
dearest child!

That's my father?
No such thing!
Father died-
Away last spring!

Father didn't die,
You dub!
Father joined the
Fishing Club!

But now there's
nowhere left to roam.
So that's why
He's here at home.

Kiss him!
He won't bite
you child!
All those fishermen look so wild!

Marie S. Cook
As told to her son Steve Cook, as a child.

PART I

New Jersey

LOVE ON THE ROCKS

By Paul Haertel

It was early June of 2003 when I and a group of avid surfcasters were fishing the south jetty of Barnegat Inlet just about every night. This group included notable anglers such as Fred Bogue, Chris LaGrossa, Chris Wahl as well as a couple LBI regulars. There had not been a lot of stripers around but each night a couple of quality fish were taken. This was a tight-lipped group of striper fishermen who were keeping the late night bite relatively quiet. We did not communicate with each other ahead of time; each of us just showed up to fish alone.

Paul Haertel with the 50.6 pound striper that carried a double meaning, it was his personal best and it was one he was able to share with his younger brother Carl, "He was like a son to me." He passed away a year later.

Every one of us had been using live eels for these fish that generally ranged from the high-teens to over 30 pounds. While the group remained quiet, so that the jetty would not become too crowded, most of us began fishing the jetty more frequently. The exception was Chris LaGrossa and I, as we fished each night regardless. On nights when the ocean was rough, some of us would make a dash to the end of the jetty and climb up on the cement monument. We would do this to ensure a spot atop a choice rock when the tide receded sufficiently to fish safely. This group of fishermen had mutual respect for one another. When someone hooked up, the others would stop fishing until the fish was landed and there was always someone willing to help out when needed.

I had taken a few fish during the week but was unable to catch one over 30 pounds. However, on one particular night I lost a really good fish. It felt heavy initially but then charged the jetty at full speed. This is something that some really big fish have done to me in the past. Unfortunately, this particular striper wrapped around a submerged rock that was nearly at my feet and then headed east like a freight train. I quickly back-reeled while twitching my rod tip in a frantic attempt to free the line, however, my efforts were for naught as the line frayed and broke.

The following night the forecast was for northeast winds that would increase as the night wore on. As I recall, it was cool and drizzling as I walked to the jetty around midnight. However, since the wind was not yet too bad, I was quite surprised to find myself alone on the jetty. I thought perhaps something was wrong since nobody else was there but it was quite fishable. The ocean was choppy and there were some swells as the current was ripping into the inlet.

I tried fishing my eels in the inlet for about half an hour and had one hit but I missed it. I repositioned myself onto an end rock on the ocean side of the jetty so that I could cast into the ocean. On my second cast, I had a soft hit and hooked a bass that initially felt small as it just stayed still and thrashed around a little bit. However, it then charged the jetty at incredible speed three different times before turning around and heading back out. Then all of a sudden it took off like a bat out of hell and headed at a 45-degree angle towards the beach while peeling line out against drag at an alarming rate.

By now I knew I was into a good fish but still did not think it was anything really special. As I picked up my gaff and began following the fish toward shore I was happy that the fish had gone that way since it was actually calmer on the ocean side of the jetty and it would be easier to land the fish there. I gained some line back but then disaster nearly struck. The bass had turned to the south and made it's way over to the old submerged south jetty. I felt it rubbing my line on the rocks and once again I had to back reel to try to keep the line from breaking.

The fish then tangled my line in the rocks and I would gain a little line and then the fish would take it back. I put a bare minimum of pressure on my rod as I walked halfway back to the beach where I tried to free it again to no avail. At this point, I considered breaking it off but instead decided to walk in even closer to the beach. I was only about thirty yards from the beach when my line miraculously came free. I knew my line had been severely frayed from the ordeal and I also knew that this was a heavy fish as I cautiously worked her toward me.

Then the fish took off again heading east along the jetty. I scrambled after her and ended up perched upon a slanted rock that stuck out further into the ocean than the others. I worked the fish closer and shined my light on it for a second when it was about 40 feet away. I figured that it was in the 30's but I did not get a good look at it. I turned the light on again a few moments later as a wave pushed it to my feet. I missed a grab as it was pushed partially under the rock I was standing on. I did not miss on my next attempt and finally hoisted her up. I looked around and could not figure out how I ended up getting onto the rock I was now on without falling. There was no way I was letting go of this fish now. I eventually made it back onto the top of the jetty. I carried the fish back out to the monument and secured it.

In the past I had caught several bass over 40 pounds and I suspected that this one exceeded the 50-pound mark that every surfcaster strives for. Still, I couldn't just leave! I knew from experience that on those rare nights when there were big bass around that there could be an even bigger one out there. I then stripped off some of my frayed line, took a short break and began fishing again. By now the wind had increased and the waves had really begun to kick up so after another half hour I happily called it a night.

The next day I was accompanied by my younger brother Carl as I proudly drove to various sport shops where I had entered tournaments. I ended up winning several awards for this fish, the largest and most prestigious being the $1000 cash first place prize for LBI's Simply Bassin' Tournament. I am glad that my brother Carl was there to share those moments with me. He was like a son to me and he passed away unexpectedly just one year later. The bass weighed 50 pound 10 ounces and it remains as the largest I have caught to this day.

GENERATOR HOLE

By Jim "Murty" Murtagh

"My father and I did a lot of stuff together…he was my best friend!"

It was 1983 or 1984 and I was just getting into surfcasting on my own, I had been allowed to go with my dad as a kid when there was room in his buddy's buggy. I did not have a great deal of knowledge but I was game for anything. I bought an 11-foot Fenwick from a guy named Fred Hoffman who was a distance caster, a Penn 750ss and loaded it with 20-pound Ande mono. For the four years prior I had been fishing freshwater bass tournaments and fishing was no longer fun. I just wanted to fish without all the pressures of competition.

At the time, everyone was mostly fishing for bluefish, stripers were not common. The few times I was on the beach at low tide there was this old man out on the bar casting a hi-lo rig and catching blackfish with bait that he would dig in the sand. I used to watch him, but tried to be respectful and not bother him, I saw he was digging sand bugs. I figured this was my chance. So I introduced myself and offered to dig bait for him if he would tell me how to find and rig the sand bugs.

He said he would be happy to let me dig bait for him! His name was John and he usually fished with his friend Mike, they would only fish at low tide so they could dig fresh bait and reach the spot that held the tog. I was only lucky enough to fish with Old John and Mike for two years. I don't remember who got sick first, but when one stopped fishing it was not the same for the other. I never saw either one again.

This spot that we fished was just like any other sand beach in Jersey, no rocks, no boulders, no jetties, just sandy beach. For two years, I would put on my new, top-of-the-line Red Ball waders, and hump my gear, rod, bag, shovel, bucket, spike and small cooler for brewskies about 400-yards down the sand and look for the two flag poles that you had to line up in order to find the old generator. The generator came out of one of the old, oceanside hotels, they dragged out into the surf, that was how they got rid of it I guess. The generator held the blackfish.

The tog fishing was great, many times my Dad and I would get 10 to 15 fish each averaging 8 to 10 pounds. There were not as many people surf fishing back then but the folks who saw us dragging nice tog off the beach were interested in what was going on. At times it got crowded, two or three other guys was crowded back then and I had to use my secret weapon to clear them out prior to fishing. I was told never to tell or show anyone this spot. The secret weapon of the day was a boom box, (another 10 pounds to drag down the beach) with some Redbone blasting and a freshwater setup with a spinner bait. After ten minutes of the music and me casting the spinner bait all over the place everyone left and it was clear to fish. This worked every time.

One Sunday afternoon low tide was at 3 p.m., the wind was out of the west and the moon was full the night before. I got to the beach before two, the only people on the beach were surfing and not even close to the Generator Hole. Great, I can leave the boom box in the truck. I dug up a bucket of the biggest sand bugs I have ever seen. I rigged up and walked into the trough to get to the bar. On my second step I was in water up to my neck (it was necessary to pass through the deep trough to get to the bar). With my waders full of water, I figured, "Well, I'm wet anyway I will keep going to the bar and cast for the other side of the world." I got back to dry land, spiked the rod and figured the waders would act like a wetsuit and warm the water so I didn't worry about it.

Looking at the rod tip for the signs of a bite, I had timed my first cast just right. The blackfish seemed to circle the generator and after hooking the first fish you could almost set your watch for the next hit. The rod tip bounced sharply one time. Then about three seconds later the fish got the bait in the back of the mouth to the crusher plate and the rod went down hard. The fish was only about 7 pounds. I got it over the skinny water on the bar and to the beach with no problems. I put a new bug on, checked to make sure I was in position with the flag poles and out onto the bar for another cast I go. The water in the trough was not as deep now because the tide had begun to really drop out and I got to the bar with little trouble.

Back on the beach, I spiked the rod and saw my dad walking toward me with his gear. I waved to let him know that the fishing was good. While I was waiting for dad to get down the beach I figured that with the tide out I would take some time to get some of the water out of my waders. Off with the belt and with the waders down around my ankles I heard my dad yelling at me.

I looked up and my rod tip was about even with the horizon. I waddled like a duck over to the rod and tried to pull the waders back on at the same time but I could not get the rod out of the sand spike with one hand. The hell with it, I figured I'm already wet and this fish is big so I'm going in like this. I dropped my waders and used two hands to pull the rod toward the water, knocked the spike down and got the rod out. This fish was huge, I think. It took about 50- to 70-yards of line against the drag. I had never felt a tog fight like this before.

Finally I had the fish close to the bar but it did not want anything to do with the skinny water and ripped another run to the north. I had to try to follow it with my waders still down around my ankles. I figured I would try and kick my waders off like a pair of sneakers, but because of the water they stick and will not budge. Things were not going well, but I was not going to lose this fish!

Into the water I went, walking like a drunken duck and like before, the first step was the deep one and head first into the drink I went. I tried to keep the reel out of the water and stand up at the same time. No good with the reel, but I managed to stand up and get to the bar. Finally, I get the fish to the bar and see that they are both hooked very well and this is why I did not lose them. Yes, I said they. It was a double header, one big fish swimming one way and one smaller fish swimming the other way.

I took a couple deep breaths and turned to see if anyone was watching. I didn't see anyone not even my Dad. I wiped the salt out of my eyes and saw him rolling on the ground laughing so hard I thought he was having a heart attack. He stood up and started clapping and giving me the one finger salute. After laughing at me and busting my chops about providing free entertainment he finally came out to give me a hand. One fish was about 4 pounds and we let it go. The other was the biggest either one of us had ever caught!

We fished until dusk with a steady pick of tog. It was a Sunday and all the shops were closed. So I put the fish in a cooler in the back of my truck with a saltwater and ice mix. I had to work the next day and could not get to the weigh station until 4 p.m. While at work I checked the fish every two hours and added ice as needed. The fish was in good shape, better than me, when I finally got it to the weigh station. It weighed 14.6 pounds.

That old generator got covered up the next year in a big nor'easter. I have gone back quite a few times with no luck. It must be under a ton of sand or has been moved out of casting range by the ever-popular beach replenishment project. That old Penn 750ss still sits on a shelf in my office, the Fenwick unfortunately was stolen out of the back of my truck a few years back and Dad went up to fish with his old buddies on Christmas Eve of 2007. Boy do I miss him.

DELAWARE RIVER STRIPERS

By Mark Jolliffe

This story comes from the mid-1980's. It was in my younger days and I had been out late enjoying the night life and it was getting to be early in the day so figured that I since I was up I might as well gather my fishing stuff and head out to the mighty Delaware for some striper fishing. I had been fishing hard that week, the fishing was good, using whatever bait I could conjure up, perch, river trout, sunnies, it didn't matter, anything I could get my hands on. I remember it was a beautiful June day and I noticed that the river had good color, it was green, I associate that with good fishing as opposed to the tan water which was cloudy and translated to lesser success.

I walked down along the river to the steep bank, I climbed down the rocks, lugging all my gear with me, it was a pain, but I had to do it of course. I carried one 5-foot rod for catching bait and a 9-foot rod for the stripers and my tackle box. To get to my favorite spot I then had to wade out about 30 feet through waist deep, hard pulling current to a small rocky island.

I got there and I got ready, I had great expectations!

While rigging up, it didn't take me long to realize that I had forgotten my %@#& worms, I left them in the truck. After looking all around for something I could use, I finally found a shriveled up worm on a hook that I had left over from another trip in the bottom of my tackle box. I mean this thing looked like a peace of bacon. Anyway, I figured what the hell I'll use it and I tied it on. Soon after I caught an eel and it was perfect, around 14-inches long, I immediately rigged it on the 9-footer and tossed it in the current to let it drift down to some deeper water.

As soon as the bait settled it was picked up and I wrestled in a nice 17-pound bass, I released it and inspected the eel, it looked good, still alive, I tossed it in again. In short order it came, bam, another one! Another good fight and I finally got her in, another high-teen bass probably around 18 pounds this time. I released her also and again inspected the eel. Remember the river pulls extremely hard so each fish is a true battle. This time it looked dead I mean real dead, chewed up and spit out. So I figured it was all I had so what do I have to lose? I tossed it out again to the same place. And BAM! Again this time it was snatched up immediately, I mean as soon as it hit the water I was on. This fish took off and another good fight took place, it was another good bass, this time it was in the low-20s, I was pumped!

The problem this time was my small friend the eel was nowhere to be seen, I was done but how could I ever complain, it was a beautiful day on the river and I took three good bass. I packed up and headed for home it was a morning that I couldn't beat.

It was a similar morning when I was fishing one of wing dams on the Delaware. It was the second week of June, 1997. I always gauged the fishing for stripers by how many sunnies were schooled up in the little pocket of the wing dam near the shore. If there was a lot that meant the stripers were in thick, I think these little guys would hide there to stay out of harm's way.

On this day it was loaded so my excitement ran high. I was going to catch a couple to live-line. Well believe it or not, I tried for an hour but couldn't catch one, I was frustrated! Finally I said I am going to go out to where the water dumps around the end of the dam and try there. Well sure enough I get this huge sunny, it was bigger than my hand, a terrible bait, I threw it in the bucket anyway just in case. I kept trying for a smaller one for half hour but still no luck!

"Screw it!" I said. I took the big one out of the bucket and rigged it onto a 5/0 Eagle Claw hook with a wire leader. I incidentally started using wire and I found it had no impact on the fishing in the river and it actually gave me a little more protection from the rocks, so I kept using it.

So I got ready to cast and oops I got off a bad cast, the sunny slipped, went only 15 feet but the current caught it and pulled it quickly down stream, I left the bail of my Penn 704Z open and pinched the line with my left hand, the sunny ended up in a small tidal pool down on the left about 40 feet and I decided that I needed to reel in and re-cast.

It was at this point when I suddenly saw a torpedo heading right for my bait, I quickly closed my bail and waited to see what would happen next.

A big fish immediately hammered the sunny and headed right for the rapids where it took off downstream, the line dumped off my spool, I tighten my drag just a bit as I watched and held on. After a run of about 125 yards, the big fish hit a pool, probably to rest, and I was able to see it zig-zagging on the surface. She then went back into the rapids and further down she went.

She stopped and I finally began to work her back up river, an extremely tough task. It took what seemed like forever, I had to walk far to the left to get her into an area of calmer, slower water. I was able to do this and I got her half way up to me…that was when she turned and ran again, all the way back down to where she was originally. Here we go again. I again work her back up in the same fashion, trying to keep her far left in the slower water and up she came…reluctantly!

It took a while but finally I got her up to where I could see her, I saw the stripes on her side, it was, as I had figured, a huge and beautiful striper. I kept working her up until I could almost grab her. It was at this point that I saw my hook just barely caught in her bottom lip and I freaked, I didn't want to lose her now!! I sat down and carefully worked my way down to the bottom of the dam and then pulled the fish towards me, I grabbed her and pulled her to me, we were both exhausted!

I held her up and admired her, I leaned her up against my rod to get the length and then I took her down back into waist deep water and I stayed with her for about 15 minutes. Her dorsal fin finally stood up and life came back into the exhausted fish. I let go and she was gone. The honor was mine.

I gathered my things and headed off to work. When I got to work I told the tale of the big striper. One of my buddies measured my rod and the fish was 46 ¼ inches, even I was impressed, a damn good fish by any standard!

* * *

It was a warm day in March and I was working the river for some walleye, it always felt good to get fish that early in the season. Well this one day I came up the bank of the river and was walking on the pedestrian path that runs beside the Delaware-Raritan Canal when suddenly something in the canal caught my eye. What the heck was it?

Upon closer examination I see this huge tiger musky (Muskellunge) just cruising along the surface, it was out about two-feet from the bank and was thing was over 5-feet long! This thing was mean looking and cruising along as if to say, hey this is my space, like he was almost talking to me. A real bully!

I was like "Wow! This is so cool!" The fish just stayed up on top swimming along as I walked. I just had to show somebody, but there really wasn't anybody around. Suddenly I saw this teenage girl walking along and I called her to come here. She did the right thing and hesitantly came near, I again told her to come and look at this as I pointed into the water. Finally I guess she realized that I wasn't a weirdo and came close and I showed her the big musky, needless to say she was in shock. I could tell by the way she yelled, "Oh my god!!"

We followed the fish for what seemed like a half hour when suddenly the fish must have got tired of showing off and in one powerful stroke of the tail and in the blink of an eye the fish was gone. It was amazing sight.

SHARK WEEK!

By Nick Honachefsky

It's a mission of mine to squeeze every ounce of challenge from the surf, and in 2009, I found a new one – big time. During the first week of August, the sun was setting over the house rows on Normandy Beach, the sunbathers trodding back over the dunes to their houses for dinner, and the full moon was rising high in the sweaty summer sky. If my calculations and surf studies were correct, my bud Mickey and I were in for some monsters tonight.

If summertime swimmers only knew what swam in the shallows under the cover of darkness.....

For the past five or so years, I had been night chunking and every now and then, would get heart-stopping hits that would literally bend the 12-foot rods right at the butt section and then the line would inevitably snap from the force of the first take. This time we were prepared with wire leaders and size-12/0 octopus hooks, it was time to go toe-to-toe with the unseen.

We set out with heavy duty 12-foot chunking rod and reel setups, a cooler full of fresh bunker, and a 5-gallon bucket of bunker chum. That's right, chum. It wasn't cow stripers or bluefish we were after, but sharks, not the puny "nuisance" smooth dogfish that one thinks of during summer nights, but true surf bruisers – browns, duskies, hammerheads and spinner sharks. We baited up half bunker pinned onto the huge hooks and cast them into the placid, moonlit, windless surf.

I cracked a beverage, took a sip and said, "Hey Mick, get ready, I know they're here."

Within 15 minutes, it all unfolded. BAM!

"Fish on! Fish on!"

My rod was bent the likes of which would break a normal surf stick in two. I grabbed the rod out of the spike and held on tight. Braided line was screaming off the Penn 6500 reel, hundreds of yards were melting off the spool at an astounding rate, I was lucky to stop this fish before running out of line! Running down the beach, I tried to gain line and stay in front of him, when he made another scorching run. After 20 minutes of battle, the headlamps were shined into the undertow where a ghostly reflection of eyes came shining back.

"Shark, man, shark!" Mickey yelled.

Mickey ran down in the undertow, grabbed the wire leader, and dragged up a 75-pound brown shark, snapping teeth and all.

"Oh man, it's on! Your rod! Your rod!" I screamed and pointed.

Mickey's rod had been launched out of the sand spike and was being dragged into the surf, we could only see the bright fluorescent green cyalume light of the rod tip entering the water.

Mickey rushed to the rod, picked it up and held on for the proverbial sleigh ride, setting the hook and running down the beach to stay in front of it. The game of give and take was on for 15 minutes when Mickey pulled in a snapping 55-pound dusky shark.

"This is unreal!" Mickey exclaimed exasperated.

For the next three hours, we bailed one shark after another, beaching 16 out of 28 hookups. Browns, duskies and spinner sharks were all caught and released. The following three nights after the full moon was absolutely mind-boggling. We landed a total of 56 sharks out of 92 hooked, with sharks ranging up to 110 pounds and 6 feet long!

The thrill of surf sharking will no doubt be gaining a following in the upcoming years. What really drives me to keep coming back is to see the ones we didn't, or simply, couldn't land. Reports were heard of boaters catching hammerheads, threshers, mako's and great whites only a few-hundred yards off the beach in 2009. With some of our hits simply spooling 400 yards of braided line off in less than 10 seconds, there's no doubt we had some true surf beasts hooked. The midsummer full moon truly does mark Shark Week in the surf. Is it possible? Surf makos? I'll find out this year.

A SURFCASTER'S MEMORIES FROM LONG BEACH ISLAND

By Bob Misak

The Long Beach Island (L.B.I.) Surf Classic is a south Jersey novelty. This striped bass and bluefish tournament runs for eight weeks every year from the first week of October through to the first week in December. L.B.I. certainly had its share of weird happenings; here are just a couple that have taken place. These stories are accurate and real with no embellishments added.

Each year the extravaganza brings between 900 and 1000 entrants to Long Beach Island to fish, with this many people it is inevitable that strange happenings occur.

Lost and Found

In 2006 there was the untimely story of Pete Figeuroa, a sharpie who looks forward to fishing the "derby" every year. He set out on a normal day to try his hand at jumping on top of the leader board, setting up his two rods in his spikes and waiting for the "big hit". He waited and waited, and as we all tend to do when things are slow, we tend to focus our attention on other things, such as a fox looking to do some bait stealing or seeing a couple gulls fighting over a bunker head. As Pete somehow became distracted, the "big hit" came and his rod was yanked out of the spike as fast as you can say, "Boo!" It was dragged into the surf…gone!

Well Pete chalked it up as a loss only after some local surfers did their best to try to spot his rod. They said the rod flew so far through the air that you couldn't have thrown it that far if you tried. After about three days a boater came in with a rod he had snagged over a mile out in the ocean. As he pulled in his line, on one end was Pete's rod! On the other, a 54-inch bass! With the winning fish that year weighing 39 pounds it is fairly safe to say that Pete probably had the tournament winner which would have put him into the money. The fellow that hooked Pete's rod tracked him down and returned the rod, but it was much too late to return the fish. Strange but true!

Goodbye Gaff

In 2007 another regular of the L.B.I. Surf Classic suffered a similar fate; Kevin Wong, a good friend of mine and an awesome fisherman, reluctantly went out on the "south jetty" to try his luck for a big cow. He hooked up and fought his mega-bass for over 20 minutes, having the gaff at his feet for when he got his chance to land the monster. The raging currents that make this place a good fishing spot, have also spelled disaster for many anglers who were trying to land their trophy. Kevin certainly had his hands full!

He saw the fish. It was 50 easy! He got the fish next to him and reached down for the gaff. There were guys there to gaff the fish for him, but as per the rules of the tourney he had to land it alone. With some friends looking on, Kevin sunk the gaff. The fish was so heavy that when he pulled on the gaff his feet went right out from under him, landing him on his keester. The line broke and the big mama bass swam out into the ocean with the gaff handle sticking out of the water until she disappeared. Kevin, being the die hard that he is came back in 2008 and redeemed himself with a 40-pound fish that took home the whole "grip of cash." The moral of this story; when you lose a bass of a lifetime, don't dwell on it. Move on to the next fish and try not to give it another thought. Kevin Wong is one of the few I know of that can actually do that! Strange but true!

Killer Sheepshead

I was fishing the tip of Barnegat Inlet's south jetty on L.B.I. when I hooked into a giant sheepshead. I was fishing with my friend Jason Close, who lives every waking moment to catch fish. As I honed in on the sheepshead, it just kept ripping out line. As the big bruiser started to tire I attempted to lift it over a high rock to get it up on top of the jetty. As it slid over the rock, the line snapped and the fish was lying sideways on the rocks below me.

Jason dropped his rod and jumped down on the low-lying rock with a giant wave rolling in. I yelled at Jay to let the fish go. He reached down and jammed his thumb into the fish's mouth and the sheepshead crushed down on his thumb with its razor sharp teeth. Jay, screaming in pain, lifted the big sheepshead up and flopped it at my feet (thumb still in it's jaws) and was then blasted by the rogue wave.

Still screaming in pain he climbed up and it took a half a minute or more to pry the sheepshead off his thumb leaving what I thought would be some permanent scars on his thumb. That's a real friend, risking a body part to save a fish from getting away. The sheepshead now hangs proudly upon my wall at 14 pounds, 3 ounces and for the fun of it I stuck a fake finger into its mouth! (Just kidding, I wouldn't do that to my buddy Jason.) Strange and crazy, but oh so true!

State Record Trigger…By a Nose!

I was cruising up and down Long Beach Island on a summer day looking for some place to do some fishing and I decided to stop at Barnegat Light Bait and Tackle. As I pulled into the parking lot I saw a guy getting ready to fillet what looked to me like a big trigger fish. I immediately jumped out of my truck and ran over to the man and asked him, "Did you weigh that fish?" As he told me he didn't, the fish flipped on the table. I said to the man, Ron Pires, "this fish is still alive. How long ago did you catch it?" He said the fish was lying on the deck of his boat for over half an hour.

I grabbed the fish and brought it to the spot tank in the back of the store. The fish uprighted itself after some assistance and was swimming heartily in the tank. After the fish was safe and alive we weighed it and found it to be a state record by one ounce. We put it back in the tank and instantly called Jenkinson's Aquarium in Point Pleasant, N.J. on the boardwalk. Lonnell, who is the fish doctor up there, told us to bring it in and she would prepare an isolation tank just for Ron's beautiful catch.

After submitting the paperwork to the state claiming the new record catch, Ron and I and the guys from the shop filled up a big tank and we started our long journey from L.B.I. to Point Pleasant on a weekend in the middle of summer. After about an hour and a half we finally made it to the aquarium. Lonnell was waiting with a 150 gallon isolation tank where she quarantined the trigger and gave it medication to heal the wound from the hook. The fish is now officially the new state record and anyone who wants to visit the giant trigger that weighed in at 5-pounds, 14 ounces can go to Jenkinson's Aquarium and enjoy the sight of this majestic tropical beauty! So close to being on the dinner table only to end up with a life of luxury! Strange, but true once again!

Old Dumb Luck

I remember sitting in the Barnegat Light, NJ tackle shop one late afternoon with the shop manager, Josh Falcone. Things were slow on the beach and we were waiting for a fresh load of bunker to arrive so we could try to entice some of the bigger bass that were around. Outside a car pulled up with a fellow holding an old, beat up Berkeley Buccaneer (you know, "the banana stick") rod with an old Penn Squidder reel on it and it is sticking out of his open window. The guy walks into the shop and says, I'm Pat, and I want to go fishing on the surf but I can't get this rod apart."

Josh and I went outside, he grabbed one end and I grabbed the other and we pulled and pulled until I pulled the bottom eye of the rod halfway off. After taping the eye back on with some electrical tape we got the rod apart and slapped some oil on it and then I pulled on the drag. I said "the drag works and the line seems strong, but this rod came from a garage somewhere and hasn't been used in years. Pat told us it was his dad's rod and he did indeed pull it out of hiding. We asked him if he wanted to wait for fresh bait and he said he'd take the old stuff. As he walked out and drove off, we laughed, thinking we had a nut in the store.

I got my fresh bunker and took off up to the sands and hit a good hole in the Barnegat Light area. As I walked up over the hill I saw a guy fishing in two feet of white water and next to him was a giant lump on the beach that looked like a tree stump. You know where I'm going with this right? I walked down the hill and over to the dude and low and behold it was Pat. He was sitting on his bucket fishing and laying next to him, a giant cow. I put the fish on my scale and it tapped out at 36 pounds,10 ounces. Pat said to me, "what do you think my chances are of catching another one of these things?"

I was speechless for the first time in my life. I congratulated Pat and from that day forth he was adorned with the affectionate nickname, "Dumb Luck Pat," which he proudly accepts because of the way he taught Josh and I a lesson. And Josh and I have learned not to be so hard on the greenhorns, for our own sakes.

Stories like this are the ones that bring me out day after day to search out the unusual, not surprisingly, I almost always find the unusual. I wonder what the next crazy occurrence I will run across on my travels up and down south Jersey, and look forward to see something odd just when I think I've seen it all. Good luck and "crazy fishing" to everyone.

The Dancing Pumpkin

Long Beach Island's Fall Surf Classic, typically runs for eight weeks, from October to the end of November, and there are many alternative prizes that anglers shoot for. One is called the "dancing pumpkin," which features a dancing pumpkin on the web site and is worth $125.00 to the closest bass to 17 pounds on Halloween day. Since I was lucky enough to win the prize in past years I decided I would do a Halloween chase for the cash.

I arrived early in the morning on the beach in Brant Beach to one of the hot bass spots that had a huge trough running along the beach. As I stuck my rods in their holders I backed up and stepped right into the trough. There was no warning, I was soon hearing the bubbles of the white water slamming against my ear drums. As I surfaced with one of my not so cheap rods still in hand, I said, "It's a pagan holiday. This is supposed to happen." Yeah right. Well, if you're a surf guy and you don't carry a change of clothes with you you're nuts.

So I went back to the truck, completely changed into dry clothes with the exception of my water-filled waders, that I hung up to dry, and began to warm up. I quickly shoved on my knee boots and walked back to the trough thinking that I wasn't being too smart, but also thinking about all the crazy stuff about being persistent, working hard. I spend so much time on the beach I should just bring a tent with me and I set up camp. I re-chunked my rods and cast them into the water.

As I hung around waiting for my waders to dry out and trying to keep warm, my one rod got whacked. I set on the fish, and carefully guided the fish to the edge of the trough. The fish was a nice 10-pound blue and I was happy to see that fish were in the area. As I unhooked the blue and released it the other rod went down and I hooked up again, I was starting to think that I was in for a gator-fest but I got the fish closer and its shiny stripes caught my eye. I got the bass up and weighed it, 17-pounds 2 ounces the scale read. The dancing pumpkin was mine!

Persistence is the best teacher I know when it comes to bass fishing and being a little stubborn along with it, can make for terrible recipe for success. On this day all it cost me was a bunker and a load of laundry. I still fish for that dancing pumpkin every year.

The Hat

It seems that almost all the anglers I know have some type of hat or other lucky item that they think is the reason why they do so well catching fish. I was at a church bazaar with a friend of mine, Bill Dawson. As we walked through the tables, I noticed some real nice wool hats that looked like they would be warm on the beach. Bill says to me, "why don't you buy one of those? Maybe it will bring you some luck." I told Bill I wasn't a particularly religious kind of guy but I went ahead and bought the hat anyway.

I went to the beach to fish the next morning and of course with the words of my Christian friend ringing in my head, I put the hat on. I set up on the sand and nailed two 20-pound bass instantly. Could it be that the hat was doing it?

For the next week or two I went everywhere with that hat on and never got skunked, not even once! I was nailing 12- to 15-pound blues and bass every time I hit the beach. I decided to take the hat on a turkey hunting trip to put it to the ultimate test. That morning I harvested a trophy turkey. It seemed as though I could do no wrong while wearing my heavenly hat that I had bought from the church.

One day I decided to fish in a harsh northeast storm up on an open sand bar in the Barnegat Light surf. I was tossing bunker with 10-ounces of weight and they were drifting down the beach like nobody's business. I slammed one giant blue after another and then a bass, then another big blue, then another bass. I was in a frenzy!

As I was fighting fish, working up a good sweat, I ripped off the hat and shoved it into my pocket trying to keep from over-heating. As I got a break in the action I began to get cold and reached into my pocket for my hat. It was gone. The wind was so fierce that it ripped my lucky hat out of my pocket or maybe I missed the pocket when I shoved it in there. I stood on the beach in a raging nor'easter, totally thinking that I would never catch another fish as long as I lived because my hat was gone.

I caught something dark out of the corner of my eye. Down the beach about 40 yards was my hat, washing in and out of the surf. I took off towards it swearing that I would save it or go down with it!

As I closed in on 20 yards away from the hat, out of nowhere, this big seagull swoops down, grabs onto the hat like a chunk of bait, flies out about 80 yards and drops the hat into the ocean. I watched as the hat disappeared beneath the water and I walked back to my rods. I dejectedly re-baited my rods and sat down on my bucket, convinced that my life as a fisherman was now over. I looked up and my rod was cranked over and the bait runner was spinning like a top. I hooked up with what turned out to be a 31-pound, 8-ounce bass. I thought of the significance of the hat and why I had so much faith in that thing.

That dumb hat made a better fisherman out of me because of the simple fact that I felt invincible with it and it pushed me to fish longer and harder, which is probably the reason I went to fish in a 40 mph blow. So, do good luck charms work? In more ways than you think. I have a new "lucky hat," and it works just as well as the last one however I did buy it at the church.

The Farmer

A young fellow was fishing a farm pond near his home and he hooked into a huge largemouth bass. As he got the fish close to shore, an eagle picked up the bass and dropped it onto a farmer's property next to the pond. As the man was climbing the fence to retrieve his trophy, the farmer pulled up in his tractor. The farmer said, "what are you doin' on my property?" The man said he wanted to get his bass. The farmer told the man, "Around here, we settle things by going punch for punch." The man, looking at the feeble old farmer said, "Okay, you go first." The farmer got off his tractor and drilled the guy right between the eyes, knocking him down. The man staggered to his feet and said, “Nice punch. Now it’s my turn.” The farmer looked at the man and said, “Nah, I quit. You can have your fish.”

This is not a true story, but it is as unbelievable as the true accounts depicted in this chapter. Good luck and great fishing.

AN EPIC SURPRISE

By DJ Muller

The epic fish that came as an 'epic surprise.' DJ Muller thought for sure he had an easy 40 that evening.

It was 2006 and the good times had come back to the Garden State in the terms of striped bass fishing. For a few years previous the adult menhaden had made a mighty return to the shallow waters of New Jersey and its beaches. The time period from May until early July gave the surfcaster a legitimate shot at hitting a bass that up to that point was only available in dreams! After all it was in the 80's that we almost said good-bye to the striped bass completely. If it were not for the action and sacrifices made by the many involved, the striper could well have disappeared altogether. Now it was the complete opposite, there were bass all over and large were common.

Let me explain to you what the common scenario was. Huge schools of adult menhaden would swim into the shallow waters of the northern Jersey beaches. This type of action ranged basically from the bottom of Long Beach Island all the way north to Sandy Hook—the northern third of the Jersey coastline. With the bunker, as the menhaden are commonly known, came huge bass, bass exceeding 50 and 60 pounds and probably bigger, they averaged between 25 and 35 pounds.

Almost without warning, the bunker would come to the beach, I mean right into the trough, hot on their tails where striped bass and sometimes big bluefish. There would be times when the bass would launch all-out attacks on these schools causing all hell to break loose. Any surfcasters in the vicinity, providing their equipment was adequate, would cash in with stripers that would make any surfcasters season highlights and maybe even career highlights.

It was late-afternoon approaching dusk when I drove down a quiet street and up to the beach. A beautiful summer's evening had brought out hordes of beach-goers, joggers, tourists and bicyclists, it was just that time of year. Upon getting to the boardwalk rail, I immediately noticed a huge school of bunker down in the wash 100 yards from where I stood, I knew I had to act quickly so I hustled back to my truck and geared up as fast as I could.

Waders: check! Wader belt: check! Plugbag: check! Camera: check! Rod and reel: check! I was good to go. Off I went and to my delight the fish had held in the vicinity. Sometimes they would come into the wash, but by the time you got geared up, they would be long gone with no return eminent.

I had a good bass on my first cast, the kind of start I like! These were all good-sized bass too mind you, small bass don't chase the huge bunker, and some of these went better then 2-1/2 pounds. The bass were big, hungry, aggressive fish. If you give one of these fish a good presentation, you would be rewarded with a nice fish in short order.

My drag zipped as I watched my rod double under strain. After some back and forth I had a bass of about 22 pounds on the beach, I quickly unhooked it and released it. After my release I couldn't help but notice the amount of bunker and the size of the bunker that were off to the right of me. Seeing the swimming-pool-sized dark stain of a bunker school within casting range is one thing, but seeing the same school with huge bass blowing through it is quite another!

The surf-line was now dotted with surfcasters, many engaged, but it was in no way shoulder to shoulder not even close, plus the school of bait and fish were spread over a three block area. I hooked and landed a couple more low-30 pound bass and I walked south toward a pronounced pocket of heavy surface action. Upon my arrival, bass were blowing these bunker 3- to 4-feet out of the water. I walked around the high, stubby jetty and looked further south to see a sight that would burn into my memory for the rest of my days. From where I stood to the next rock jetty, about 250 yards to my south, from where the water touched the beach and out about 40 yards, the water was solid black with anxious bunker, the bass had them hemmed in, and the sight was sobering.

On this particular day I was using a Yo-Zuri Surface Bull that I had sanded down from its original colors of pink and yellow and then re-painted a dull primer white. The original color pattern had failed me miserably in a hit of big bass a few weeks earlier. I threw the lure over and over and over with no fish while the guys to my right and left had big bass on every cast. I am superstitious like that.

I cast my lure long and retrieved it. I worked it to the back of a breaking wave and watched it as it plunged through the white water, it was sizing up to be an uncommon fishless retrieve! The lure splashed its way back to me and I readied to lift it from the wash and recast when suddenly the popper exploded in a flash of white spray. It caught me totally off guard. The fish turned and dumped line from my reel, it was the best fish I had hooked this spring and I tightened my grip on the rod and raised the tip high.

This fish was smoking my reel and my senses went to all out, I knew I had a fight coming and I was fairly certain that I hooked my first 40 of the spring, I was all jacked up as the adrenaline raged through me. The fish ran out about 75 yards and then thrashed on the surface for a couple seconds before diving and making another powerful run. "Holy shit!" I thought. This could be a 50!

I knew that if I was patient with this fish there was no way that it was going to beat me. I always re-tied all my knots to my braid and put a fresh 80 pound monofilament leader on every time I went out or got ready to go out. My duo-locks were big and new. I left no stone unturned as far as equipment. My Van Staal 200 and my 11-foot All-Star rod were up to the task, I just had to wait for this cow to tire. I relaxed as I knew I had this girl beat.

As my confidence continued to peak the big fish then made a move that I didn't figure on and I am not sure why. She made a turn and then steamed north. North right towards the jetty that I had just passed a few minutes earlier. "Oh shit!" I thought. I never even thought about the fish going that way but she did and it was full bore. She was going to go around the jetty and break me off, damn! I tried in vain to stop her or turn her but I quickly realized that there was no way that was going to happen and I followed her down the beach while formulating my next move. What was I going to do now?!

I had to either stop this fish or I would lose her to the jetty and she was too loaded up and fresh (what I call "green"), I couldn't stop her run towards the jetty so I did a quick assessment of the situation. I quickly admitted to myself that I have only one shot. How? Well where most of New Jersey's jetties are long and relatively low to the water, this "mountain" was unusually short but higher than most. I ran up behind the jetty and decided that I was going to try to lift my rod as high as I could and hopefully clear the jetty. It was a far fetched idea...but maybe!

As the fish approached the tip of the rock pile I grabbed my rod at the very end of the butt and pulled what I nicknamed, "The Statue of Liberty Play." I lifted it high over my head. I stood as high as I could on my tippy-toes, then I shot off a quick prayer to the big man as I stumbled my way around the jetty. I snicker about it now, wondering who may have been watching me and wondering what the heck I was doing.

Well believe it or not, and I still don't believe it to this day, that bass (and my line), cleared that jetty tip and the fight raged on. Now, on the north side of the jetty, the water in the jetty pocket was deep and turbid with hard pulling currents and crashing waves. I am usually not shy about going into the water to "wrestle" a fish, but this water looked just a little bit too deep and rough for my comfort zone. I couldn't risk it. I had what I had now determined was a 42-pounder (don't ask me why) on the business end and I was looking to close out this epic battle that was now approaching 10 minutes in duration. The dusky evening sky was now running to black.

I leaned back extra hard and pumped the fish to me, she was still a reluctant participant, a real warrior! At long last and fighting for every inch, I finally saw my barrel swivel but still have yet to see this "BEAST!" I couldn't wait so I carefully went into the water waist deep and grabbed the huge striper and dragged her up onto the sand, I breathed a sigh of relief and reached for the Boga Grip on my belt, I wanted to weigh this fish!

I looked hard at the small numbers on my scale, it bounced at she swung her tail 26, 32, 27, 30…it steadied…28.5 pounds! What?! No way! That's it?! I couldn't believe that a fish of this strength, that battled the way it did, didn't even break 30 pounds! I have some heavyweights under my belt and I thought for sure this one was in their class. I was in disbelief!

I finally caught my breath unhooked my trophy and quickly walker her down into the water. With the thumb of my left hand in her mouth and my right hand around her tail I steadied her in the pounding surf and gave her time to get her oxygen levels back up to where they should be and to rest for a few seconds. I stayed with her for a long while until I felt her kick. I then tightened my grip on her a little more, I wanted to be sure this one lived to swim another day. It had given me a memorable battle and I owed it to her.

After a couple more minutes and a couple waves over the noggin, she clamped down hard on my thumb and fought me. I released her tail and pushed her into the warm night-waters of early-July and watched her disappear from sight. Something deep inside me felt satisfied. I collected myself, breathed a cleansing exhale and thought about the battle, turned and headed for home. It was an epic battle that finished with an unexpected surprise.

HE SWAM WITH THE FISHES

As told to DJ Muller by Joe Pallotto

Joe Pallotto is a man that loves life and has lived life to the fullest. A loud, verbose, happy man, never short for words. He has spent a lifetime at the water. Not only did he spend his days and nights chasing striped bass and live-lining herring along the Jersey beaches but he was also a lifeguard and the Beach Director for the city of Asbury Park for over 50 years. Pallotto was a crazy striper fisherman in a high time of striper fishing. He lived in a day that on any given morning a 40- or 50- pound striper could have been sitting off a jetty tip waiting for breakfast.

He is a popular name associated with striped bass fishing and more specifically surf fishing on the Jersey Shore. He is president of the oldest saltwater fishing club in the country, the Asbury Park Fishing Club which was founded in 1889.

Here are just a few of his stories.

One day Joe was fishing the Conventional Hall jetty in Asbury Park when he suddenly tied into a good fish. The fish took off and Joe went running down the side of the jetty trying to keep up with the fish, he needed to get the fish to the other side where he could get a shot at landing it. Well as he was running he of course tripped and fell, his elbow hit a rock and his rod went flying out of his hand and landed in the water.

The second it happened and without thinking twice, he said, "Hell I ain't losin' my rod!" So he jumped into the water and grabbed the butt of the rod and started to doggy paddle while holding his rod with the fish on. His boots filled with water and started taking him down so he kicked his boots off and continued to swim with his rod and his fish.

The guys that clean the beach showed up at 6 a.m. and saw him struggling in the water. They made a human chain, got out to him and grabbed him and pulled him in…along with his 42-pound pound striper.

On another morning Joe was fast asleep in his small garage apartment on Sunset Avenue, when a fellow long-time live-liner Bud Johnson came knocking on his door at 5:30 in the morning. "Joey, I have to go to work can you do me a favor? I broke off a big fish on the end of Sixth Avenue jetty. I tied my line off in the rocks…can you go get it for me?" So Joe being the good guy he is, went down to the jetty and found the line. He dove in and swam out following the line and sure enough he found this huge bass and the bass is just sitting there. He grabbed the fish by sticking his arm through the gill plate and swam it in to the beach. The fish weighed 40-pounds. He took the bass to K&B Fish Market and sold it for 30 cents a pound. He then gave the money to Bud when he saw him later that day. (Joe jokes, "He was cheap…not even a tip.")

Joe was live-lining herring on the jetty at Whitehall Avenue in Deal. He hooked a good fish and the fish took off. On that jetty there is no beach on the north side just a high rock embankment, so he tried to walk it around the tip to the south side beach where he could land it on the sand, a common practice. As he was attempting this, the fish swam around a piling out on the tip of the jetty and he couldn't get the fish in.

He could see that it was a good fish so he said to himself, "I'm gonna jump in the water and get this son of a bitch!" So he took hold of his line, threw his rod into the water, dove in and followed his line to the fish. Sure enough it was a huge bass. He again stuck his arm in through the gill plate and swam the fish back to the jetty.

As this was taking place Bud Johnson shows up on the jetty and is wondering what the hell was going on? He saw Joe and his fish and he helped Joe get the fish up onto the jetty, then Joe went back into the water to retrieve his rod. The fish hit the scales at 47 ½ pounds.

It was the very next day that Joe and Billy McFadden were live-lining herring on the Eighth Avenue jetty in Asbury. Behind them on the beach a bunch of guys from the club were having a cookout in the parking lot of the Marine Grill Restaurant (no longer there). Joe had his herring way out there, which was something he didn't usually let happen, but on this day he was daydreaming, not really paying attention when suddenly there was a huge splash way out.

The 25-pound test Ande started dumping off his Penn Jigmaster. Everybody came running out from the parking lot. Well this big fat guy named Andy goes out in his waders and said to Joe, "Let me gaff your fish! Let me gaff your fish!" So Joe told him, "Ok I'll pull him over into the corner. Are you sure you can do this Andy?" So Andy bent over to gaff the fish and of course he missed it and fell into the water in the process. So Billy started yelling "Andy's drowning! Andy's drowning!" Joe says, "F*** him Billy! Here's the gaff, get my G** damn fish! I'll get him (Andy) as soon as we get the fish!!" So Billy gaffed the fish and threw it up on the rocks and then Joe jumped in and grabbed Andy and threw him on the rocks beside the fish. Everybody was happy!

Joe was fishing one morning with his partner "Frog" (Mike Fidek), also a lifeguard, who Joe was with the day he took a 53-½ -pounder on Marine Place in Deal. Well Joe blew his chance with a good fish and was all piping mad. He took a walk back up to his van to get another herring and to cool down.

While at his van he notices this "nut" cruising by him heading for the jetty and the guy was "marching," yes high-stepping and everything. Joe thought it was a little strange so he decided to watch and see what happened, so he went up onto the boardwalk to watch. This guy kept marching and eventually marched right off the end of the jetty and into the ocean! Joe thought to himself, "Now I know I was out drinking and partying a lot last night and maybe I am that messed up. But did I really see this?" So he turned his attention to Frog to see what his reaction might be.

So Frog was standing there live-lining away and he too sees this guy march right into the water. When he saw him go in he reeled in his herring, put it into the bucket real quick and went running over to the end jetty and looked into the water. Frog started yelling, "Joe come out here, come out here, this guy is trying to kill himself!" So Joe runs out there and said, "Frog you go in and get him and I'll go get help," Frog says, "F*** you, you're going in the water with me!"

So Frog took his pants off and he had these little white boxer shorts on and he crawls down the green, slime-covered rocks, slipping and sliding all over the place and Joe started laughing. Meanwhile this guy is under…gone! Joe saw Frog with his shorts all dirty and started laughing even harder.

So finally Joe yelled over to the next jetty where another guy was fishing a herring and yelled, "Hey, go call for help!" The guy yells back "F*** you!" (Giving him the finger). "I ain't leaving my spot!" So Joe jumped into the water with his jeans on and he and Frog swam out and got the guy up and the only way to get him back in was to swim him all the way back to the beach. By this time the beach crew had seen what was going on and called the police and paramedics. They arrived and took the psychiatric patient to the hospital where he belonged. The funniest part of the story though was that when the police showed up they busted Frog for being in his underpants!

It was a real foggy morning Joe and Frog were fishing at the "Super Jetty" in Long Branch (Atlantic Avenue, now buried). There were a bunch of guys on hand that morning as the jetty had quite a reputation. Frog got a good fish on and he said to Joe, "The f****r is under the rocks, what am I going to do?!" Joe says "Froggy, take your clothes off and go get that son of a bitch, I'll hold your rod!" So Frog stripped down, he took all off his clothes off, dove in and started following his line. Meanwhile all the guys fishing nearby were in shock watching this, Joe could hear them saying, "What the heck is going on over there?" So he gets the line out and Joe yells to him, "Come on hurry the fish is clear!" So Frog swims back in, climbs back up the slimy rocks, jumps right back into his boots and fights the fish to the beach where it weighed 30-something pounds.

It was an early summer evening and Joe was alone fishing a herring on the Fourth Avenue jetty, in Asbury, he hooked a fish that felt pretty decent and of course the "son of a bitch" goes under the rocks out deep. So Joe asked himself, "What I am I going to do now with no help?" Well sure enough, a little black kid, probably 12 years old, came walking along the jetty. Joe said to him, "Do me a favor! Don't move!! Just hold this fishing rod in your hands and keep it straight up, I'm going into the water to get this fish!" So he dove in and got the fish out, it swam away and the kid started yelling, "What do I do? What do I do?" Joe said, "Just hold still." He climbed back out of the water and finished fighting the fish. This one was only 18 pounds but it didn't get away!

Then there was the day that Joe almost met his match. *(The Deal flume was a huge oval pipe that was 6- feet in diameter, it ran about 200 yards connecting Deal Lake to the Atlantic Ocean. Herring would travel through the pipe and into the lake to spawn a couple times a year. At certain times of the year herring were abundant and could be caught with a dip net.)*

So this one day Joe decided that he was going to go into the flume at high tide to round up some herring. His plan was to drag along with him a wooden bait box that was tied around his waist with clothesline and the box would float 20-feet or so behind him, if he needed it he could pull it in.

At high tide there was only a foot of space between the surface of the water and the top of the pipe to breath and when a wave rolled it you had to breathe through small vents in the ceiling of the pipe that lead up to the street above. As he walked through the flume he would feel the herring banging against his legs. When he felt them he would lower his dip net into the school and capture a few then bring them above the surface where he would dump them into his floating bait box.

So, on this particular occasion, Joe was in the pipe gathering herring when a big set of waves came in and filled the pipe with water, top to bottom. Joe couldn't get any air! Completely underwater, Joe had to hold his breath and finally he saw the light of a blowhole up a head and he started running for it! Unbeknownst to him the bait box had floated up and gotten stuck in another hole and Joe couldn't make it.

Thinking quickly Joe reached for the knot around his waist and tried in vain to untie it, as the line had swollen in the water and the knot was too tight! Joe started to panic. In his last push for survival, the wise water rat thought quickly and pulled on the rope and in doing so he pulled himself to the hole in which the bait box was stuck and he got his air.

Needless to say that was his last trip into the flume at high tide.

By his own confession he said, "I wasn't the greatest fisherman I just knew I could get my fish!!" His motto was: "Never let a fish get away! If it is under the rocks, get it! Don't let it get away!" And he never did.

MY SURFCASTING LIFE

By Stan Dziedzic

It's New Years Day, 2010 – I have just returned home from my daily beach walk. This morning I walked the Cove at Sandy Hook, no rod or plug bag, I just reflected. The last fish I caught were on December 16th, two stripers and two herring. My sons have been after me to write about some of my fishing memories and experiences over the years, so here goes, perhaps some of the guys my age can relate to them and remember some of the things I have.

Growing up in Bayonne, New Jersey in the 40's and 50's, my earliest exposure with saltwater fishing was catching eels and crabs off the local docks. Even though my family was limited to this type of fishing because we did not own a car I fell in love with the saltwater and knew I wanted to pursue it on a larger scale. When my family purchased a car it opened up a whole new world, our fishing trips took us to places in Staten Island, Great Kills, Princess Bay, South Beach and Wolf's Pond. Our main quarry were porgies, spots or

July 1974- "My future fishing partners, sons Andrew & Matthew, with my father-in-law and myself, admiring the 48 pound bass I caught that morning swimming a bunker."

lafayettes, fluke, bluefish and once in a while an occasional striped bass. Having a car allowed us to start fishing nights also, and in winter we would make all night trips down to the Long Branch Pier to catch whiting, ling, skates, and even angler fish or monkfish at times.

We would drive to Atlantic Highlands to fish on the party boats. My favorite boat at the time was The Delmar. The captain was a colorful fellow named Al Gable. He charged my father $2.00 for my fare. We would catch blackfish, sea bass, conger eels, bergalls, and even cod sometimes along with the whiting and ling. We called the ling "shit bellies," and when you cleaned them you found out why! After the trips we would take the whiting to Leroy's Fish Market and Smokehouse on Route 36 in Leonardo. Leroy would smoke them for us for free if we gave him half the fish to sell.

In the summertime, party boats like The Delmar, The Reliable, The Happy, out of Atlantic Highlands, and The JoAnn III out of Leonardo would anchor up and chum for bluefish. The rods and reels that we used were purchased in Jersey City at a place called Davega Sporting Goods Store. I still have the rods and reels to this day. The reels were Ocean City and Penn. Sears and Roebuck also made a line of fishing products under the name J.C. Higgins. Baseball player Ted Williams was their spokesman. The line we used was made by Ashaway Line Company in Rhode Island (if I remember correctly). It was a linen-type braided line. It had to be rinsed with fresh water and dried after each trip. We used to string it up in the basement to dry on wooden pegs, back and forth across the entire length of the basement. When using this line we had to wet it before casting because it would burn the skin off your thumb if it was dry!

When I was in the 8th grade, my family moved down from Bayonne to Leonardo, New Jersey, up the block from the Leonardo State Marina and the Earle Naval Weapons Pier. After our move, our fishing expanded yet again to surfcasting. We purchased spinning rods from The Har-Lee Rod Company in Jersey City and our reels from Red's Tackle Shop in Elizabeth. The reels we used were Penn and Quick reels. The shop had a fishing club called, Red's Surf Devils. Some of the local tackle shops at the time were Julian's Bait and Tackle, in Atlantic Highlands, located on the northbound side of Route 36, Giglio's in Sea Bright, which later became my hang out, and a place I remember as Regan's Dock in Sea Bright, Paul's Tackle in north Long Branch and Jim's Tackle was next to the Long Branch Fishing Club which was run by a fellow named Joe Cisco.

The roe from blackfish was a delicacy at Jim's Tackle. When we would catch blackfish, the female blackfish eggs would be fried up right in the shop for us to eat and it was delicious! Stephen's Tackle was on Brighton Avenue and there was a tackle shop by the pier run by a fellow by the name of Inky.

Back then I fished with guys like Armand Giglio, Inky, Charlie Cooper, a great shedder crab guy and a lot of guys whose names I can't remember. One of my best friends and fishing partner was Buddy Kruse. Buddy and I worked together at the post office, and fished together for years. We fished eels at night and shedder crabs by day. My favorite though was fishing with sandworms. I would dig them on the flats in Leonardo and the sedge banks in Leonardo and Belford. When I wasn't able to dig them I would purchase them. I would catch a lot schoolie stripers off the sedge banks on the Raritan Bay in the springtime too. Oh, and then there were clams, I used them too, back then you could get three surf or skimmer clams for twenty-five cents.

As for artificials, my favorites were the Creek Chub "Surfster" and the Rebel. Tin squids and metal were also productive. The Jetties were the hotspots and would produce bass consistently. In Sea Bright there was the Sandlass Beach Club jetty, Atlantic Way, Ship Ahoy, Anchorage, Trade Winds, the Tar Jetty, the Pink Motel, Harry Zobels Boat Works and of course the sea wall. Down further to Monmouth Beach there was the sea wall, Monmouth Beach Club and "Little Monmouth" and a place called the Nun's Wall. Long Branch had the USO Beach, Joline Avenue jetty, and all the jetties that continued all the way down to the Red Church and San Alfonso's. The "T"-Jetties from Park Avenue down to Garfield Terrace in Elberon, were my favorite, then Phillips Avenue and Whitehall and on down to 8th Avenue in Asbury Park. They were all spots that produced nice bass consistently. At Sandy Hook, the Tower Jetty and the Cove were good spots when they were open to the public.

Other than targeting striped bass, in the winter we would catch whiting and ling off the jetties. Winter night fishing on the jetties was fun, especially with a fire and a bottle of blackberry brandy.

After a couple years in Germany as a member of Uncle Sam's Army it was back home for the best part of my life. I got married and experienced the birth of my two sons. The striped bass fishing was at its peak at that time and it was easy to get caught up in it. Besides putting my time in at the beach and on the rocks, I purchased a used Mirrocraft aluminum boat and motor. I remember the 3 a.m. trips out to the pound nets to scoop bunker. I recall scooping herring from the spillway at Shadow Lake and then live-lining off the rocks. It was an almost a daily thing. At one point I installed a garbage can with an aerator in my station wagon to keep the bunker and herring alive until I could get the chance to fish them.

Tallying points for my pins for the "R.J. Schaefer Fishing Contest" became the primary goal for me and a lot of other guys in our area of Jersey. We would check the standings at Giglio's every day, comparing our fish and points to other guys and clubs throughout the northeast, competing against fishermen all the way up to Massachusetts and Cape Cod. I came up a pound or two short of the magical 50-pound mark on a couple occasions.

I was able to fish before and after work as my commute was only about 10 minutes being a mailman in Red Bank. After a few seasons, this type of fishing became more and more a competition and I didn't enjoy it as much. There was a 10-fish per day limit we were allowed to sell fish back then and being able to add a few dollars for gas and tackle was very easy to do. Just about every restaurant in the area would buy the stripers from you. How much would they pay you ask? On average restaurants would pay somewhere around .35- to .50-cents a pound for whole fish, but would pay up to $2.00 a pound for fillets. We would spend the time to fillet the fish whenever possible. Some of the restaurants would make fish chowder out of the heads of the bigger bass. If we caught a couple fish in the 20-pound range and a few other smaller fish, that was some decent pocket money!

Time went by and in the early to mid 1970's my two boys were growing up and I decided that fishing with them was more important than my quest for a "Moby" striper. My cellar wall is full of photos of our fishing over the years. We fished all the jetties that I fished when I was younger before most of them were ruined by the beach replenishment and sand pumping. We went on the Magic Hour trips for whiting, mackerel and squid before they disappeared. In addition to stripers, we would catch kingfish, blackfish, fluke and Spanish mackerel (in my opinion the best tasting fish of all time!) off the jetties. After the striped bass stocks fell the bluefish were plentiful.

My boys and I spent a lot of time in our canoe fishing the lakes and ponds in New Jersey. Our family went on yearly trips to Martha's Vineyard and we continued to fish together through their high school and college years. Thankfully my boys and I have logged a lot of memories.

My sons and I are catch and release anglers now, but we do keep an occasional striper or bluefish for the barbeque. The years of liberal laws in all states along with the rod and reel and commercial fishing pressure has had an effect on the bass numbers for sure.

I remember flounder fishing in the fall and spring in the Shrewsbury and Navesink Rivers, and when was the last time blowfish were around? Fishing has changed.

My sons have families of their own now and take their daughters fishing to the places they fished as boys. I get a lot of enjoyment watching my granddaughters catching fish and adding more photos and memories to my collection. My next birthday will be number 70. I am blessed with a healthy and happy family and consider myself very lucky to have had this life experience. Fishing was not the most important thing in our family only a nice part of it. I have since taken up fly fishing, and my wife and I enjoy drifting for fluke in our boat on nice summer days, it is very relaxing. I would wish everyone the same opportunity and health to enjoy these times with family as I have.

Thank you for spending a few minutes reading this fisherman's story. Happy Fishing!

GOLF OR TENNIS, ANYONE?

By Allen D. Riley

It was October many years ago right in the midst of a terrific north Jersey striper run. Great numbers of surfcasters were working the beaches with high hopes of getting in on the action. The word was out that the stripers in the mix were many – and that some of them were huge.

There is one incident which I will never forget that happened one Saturday morning during the latter part of that month at Sandy Hook. The shoreline early that morning around sunrise was mobbed with anglers looking to get in on the hot and heavy bass action. I don't think I can ever remember more bass anglers ever being on that stretch of beach at any other time. My expectations – and those of most of the other anglers pounding the surf with me – were very high.

At that time in my surf fishing career, I wasn't the angler that I am today but I was certainly no novice. I had paid my dues, put in my time, and acquired skills over the early years that serve me to this day. Lure fishing – rather than bait – was my personal choice to get me to striper nirvana.

My equipment that morning was modest compared to what I use today, but still adequate for the task at hand. However, I was amazed at the gear that a great many other surfcasters along the shoreline were carrying. Loomis rods, Van Staal reels, and many other comparable high-end rods and reels were in evidence as were many very expensive fly-fishing outfits that I had only seen in catalogs.

Many of the veteran striper-addicted anglers in attendance had all the proper tools and accessories in addition to their rods and reels. Hand-crafted, expensive wooden plugs were as common as off-the shelf poppers and swimmers. If "matching the hatch" was the secret to hooking up that morning, someone certainly would have had the winning combination because of the plethora of lure sizes, profiles, finishes, actions, and colors that these striper sharpies were working.

I remembered thinking that more than a few of the anglers must have thought that fashion photographers would be taking cover-photos for fishing magazines that morning. Their high-priced waders, jackets, other paraphernalia, and surf bags were simply amazing. Many of these guys were walking around with $1,000 or more in equipment in their hands and on their bodies!

For all the anglers in attendance and despite the sunrise being spectacular, I was amazed that the stripers had seemingly taken the morning off. Not a single angler had any kind of bump, follow, or strike despite the impressive variety of popping plugs, swimmers, and metal lures that were being cast and worked back to the beach. Even the bluefish were conspicuously absent.

Some anglers got so discouraged that they left, hoping to luck into fish elsewhere. Most stayed, though, hoping that the fish were just late. I was just about ready to call it a morning when I realized that there was one angler fishing bait nearby. He had gone almost completely unnoticed by just about everyone along the shoreline up until that point.

When I first saw him, I couldn't understand why someone didn't notice him earlier. Certainly, he should have stood out in the assembled crowd! He was a thirty-something angler who looked like anything but a surfcaster. He didn't have waders on – only battered sneakers. He really wasn't dressed for the rather chilly morning, and what he had on were very humble clothes. But it was his fishing combo that really caught our attention. He was using an old Zebco four-foot freshwater rod with one of those odd-looking children's reels that Zebco was famous for.

He was the only angler that I saw that morning fishing bait. His bait of choice was squid: basic squid chunks – no fancy ribbon slices – cut with a rusty old knife. The single-hook rig that he used was not striper-capable by any means. A battered two-ounce bank sinker completed his pathetic rig.

I was not surprised when the amateur surfcaster had difficulty getting any kind of distance from his cast. (I attributed that to both the shortcomings of his equipment and the angler's own obvious inexperience.) Everyone one the beach was staring at this guy and holding in their laughter—this could not be real! When the bait angler placed his small combo in his rod holder – a piece of battered PVC plumbing pipe – the effect was complete.

Up to this point, no one had spoken to this one angler who chose to fish bait while everyone else – supposedly more experienced anglers – opted to work lures. Once the novelty of his efforts and his appearance wore off, anglers began to leave the beach until... Lo and behold, the Zebco rod soon afterwards was pulled out of its sand spike and was almost dragged into the ocean. When its owner gained control of the rod, it was apparent that something B-I-G was on the line. After a long and spirited fight – fought on four-pound test mono I later discovered – a keeper bass was pulled up onto the sand.

Needless to say, all of us lure anglers were amazed and speechless. Everyone, except the bait angler, who asked everyone within earshot: "What kind of fish is this, anyway?"

None of us who witnessed this humbling experience vowed to give up fishing for golf or tennis as we watched in stunned silence. But some of us – including myself – seriously thought about it!

SO CLOSE

By Geoff Turner

Geoff Turner proudly hoists his huge bass, a fish that had every reason not to be caught.

One late afternoon in the end of June 2006, my buddy, DJ Muller and I were cruising along the beach looking for schools of moose bunker in Monmouth County, New Jersey, when we came upon one that was close to the beach and looked to be nervous. It was huge and balled up in the open water between the jetties about 100-feet from shore. Suddenly, big bass started blowing the bunker up.

Frantic 1- and 2-pound bunker were leaping out of the water in an effort to escape. I'm thinking, "Yeah! This is it!"

Quickly, we parked our trucks, put on our waders, grabbed our rods and plug bags and made haste to the water's edge. I grinned at DJ and he grinned back, our eyes wide with excitement and anticipation. The few fishermen already at the scene were also on high alert and throwing big pencil poppers. DJ and I decided to use 10/0 snag trebles instead because the bunker were bunched up tight and the few anglers there were spread far apart.

Our first casts were on the mark, over and beyond the school. A few sweeps of our rods and we each snagged a bunker to live-line. Seconds later, I felt a couple of hard jolts and line started peeling out. I reared back and set the hook, hard enough to cross the fish's eyes. The initial surge was powerful as the bass ran for deeper water away from the school; it didn't feel like anything special. Initially, I assumed a high-20-pounder, but I couldn't honestly tell how big it was. I looked over and saw DJ was also hooked up as his rod was bent double. Doubleheader! Yeah, baby!

Suddenly my Suffix braided line went slack, but the line was still moving, I realized the bass was swimming towards me. I quickly started reeling in the slack and kept on cranking and cranking and cranking but nothing was happening. I was starting to think that I lost her. Disappointed, I turned to the task of reeling in the treble so I could re-cast and snag another bunker. But still the line wouldn't come in. What the hell is going on here?!! I looked down at my Penn 705Z reel and saw the line was now peeling out instead of in! I must have forgotten to tighten my drag correctly. As soon as the line became taut again, I could feel a heavy weight pulling hard into deeper water away from the shoreline. The fish was still on! I got back to the business of fighting the fish.

At this point, I saw that Muller had already landed a 22-pounder, released it and had his line back in the water, a snagged live bunker on the other end.

But wait, my next obstacle…from my left comes this eager beaver and he decides to throw over my line with his pencil popper. Arrrrgh! The big bass was now swimming to the left, toward a jetty and I was fighting to keep her away from it. I screamed and cussed at the guy to get his line off mine. He sputtered his apologies and made several clumsy attempts to untangle his line while my line was high and tight as a piano wire above him, and moving inexorably to the jetty. Finally (what seemed like a few minutes later), he untangled our lines by swinging his popper up and over my line toward himself.

Freed from unwanted human intervention, I wondered, what else could go wrong? I proceeded to slowly work the tight line back onto the reel and to pull the fish away from the jetty. The bass reacted by trying a different tactic. She swung around and ran right, back to the open water. I knew she had to be a heavy fish because she never once came up to the surface; she kept bulldogging to the bottom in an effort to find someway to break my line and free herself.

As I'm thinking there was nothing else now to stop me from landing this fish…something did! A bunker collided with my line, its mouth open and tangled itself. All of a sudden, I see this bunker riding up my line with its mouth clamped around it as I'm reeling. It flopped like crazy in the air until it stopped at the top guide of my 10-foot rod, a factory Lamiglas XS101MS. Unbelievable!! This could only happen to me! The bunker was stuck at the tip of my rod and I was unable to crank the reel anymore. I cussed like a homesick sailor as I shook the rod frantically to shake the damn thing off. Meanwhile, the big bass was putting increasing pressure on the rod as she steadfastly continued heading towards the south jetty this time. I was amazed she hadn't spit the hook out yet. She pulled some drag and that actually freed the bunker from the rod tip. I gave my rod a mighty jerk and the bunker flew off and somersaulted back into the water. Alrighty then, back to business!

At last, I was able to guide the bass carefully toward the water's edge until I could see her broad back and dorsal fin sticking out of the water. I was stunned. I screamed to Muller, "It's big!" He looked at me as if to say sarcastically, "Yeah, yeah. They're all big". "No, it's really big!" He causally looked over and then I saw his jaw drop. He looked about ready to crap in his waders.

I pulled the fish closer to the wash until I could see her big shoulders and huge eyes. Instead of calmly using the waves to place the cow onto the sand, I fell into a bit of a panic. When I felt she was close enough, I ran toward the cow, allowing slack in my line without thinking. By doing that, I neglected to keep pressure on her with my rod and left the line laying there. I realized later it was a big mistake that could have been catastrophic.

I found myself straddling the huge fish in a foot of water. I tried grip her massive lower jaw but my hands were shaking and I was having trouble controlling her. Muller recognized my predicament and took action. He ran over, expertly put his hand under a gill plate and dragged the huge bass up onto the beach.

DJ and I, along with another passer-by who had watched the whole scene unfold, stood over the bass as it lay on the hot sand. It turned out, in spite of all the obstacles that popped up during the long battle, that I didn't have to worry about losing this fish after all, as the treble was firmly buried inside the beast's huge mouth. It was the longest bass I've ever seen with an enormous girth.

"Hmmm-mmm, that looks like it could be a 50," DJ opined and the guy nodded in the affirmative. I refused to believe it. Too many anglers have fished for stripers for decades without catching even a 40-pounder, and here I am only a few years in and already hit the Holy Grail? Nah, no way. Yet it was hard to deny what was in front of me. It nearly busted my 30-pound Boga. DJ took out his Berkley digital scale and the fish pulled it down to 50.5 pounds. "Holy crap!" I said. It was huge!

We hemmed and hawed for several minutes about taking the big fish to be weighed right away. We decided to continue fishing since the blitz was still going. But after 20 minutes the activity had quieted down. Fifteen minutes later we were on our way to Scott's, a tackle shop in Bradley Beach, for the official weigh-in. I decided to call my wife as I weaved my way through traffic.

"Deb, are you sitting down?"

"I am now. Why do you ask?"

"I think I just got a 50!"

"A 50 what?"

"A 50-pound striper!!"

"Oh. I thought you were going to tell me (something important like) you won a million dollars in the lottery. Oh well. Congratulations." (Go figure.)

At Scott's, the huge bass weighed 48 pounds 3 ounces and measured 49 inches with a 29.5 inch girth. While it fell short of officially being a 50, it was still a fish of a lifetime to me…at least up to that point in time.

Apparently, word of my "50" quickly spread faster than wildfire because when I returned to the spot, there was the proverbial picket fence of anglers on the beach throwing pencils. How did they know where I caught the fish? The bass had returned and a few 20's and a couple 30's were taken. There were also numerous crossed lines and curses flying back and forth. Classic New Jersey-style combat fishing had ensued. I tried to fish but it was getting too dangerous with dozens of pencils flying together in tight space so I gave up soon after. I didn't catch any more fish that day but I could confidently say that my one fish made my day, my year, and perhaps my career? Only time will tell.

PART II

New York

The legendary Turtle Cove sits below the beautiful Montauk Lighthouse. This place is the breeding ground for story grandeur. The rocks furthest from the Light (bottom of photo) are the beginning of a stretch known as The Brown's.

A BAD DAY

By Edward M. Greenberg

"A bad day fishing is better than a good day at work."

Every fisherman knows that this old adage is true. But we also know that there are bad days and then there are truly bad days.

"A Bad Day" by definition: You can't buy a hit meanwhile the guy right down the beach from you is bailing fish on every cast.

"A Truly Bad Day" by definition: The guy down the beach is your long time fishing buddy thus assuring you that he will never, ever let you forget this day as long as you live.

I had one such "bad day," that even after many years is still stuck in my craw. It was one of those hot summer nights we all dread. There was no breeze, the humidity was about 150%, and it was way too hot to sleep. I had set the alarm to fish a high ebb tide from first light to sunrise and tried to get a couple of hours "nap time" in the interim. After a half hour of rolling around in my own sweat, I gave up and headed to the beach in the worst case scenario, I would nap in the truck, it had to be cooler at the beach. I only mention this because I'm sure the lack of sleep affected my perception of the events to come.

I arrived at the beach and quickly decided that fishing is better than sleeping so I began to fish. I was in a pretty decent high tide spot with good structure, a hole, some back eddies off the rip, and a nice sod/rock embankment. For the next hour I threw everything in my plugbag; bucktail to Bomber, needlefish to darter, without so much as a touch.

It was at this point when I noticed headlights weaving down the beach and coming my way. Now this guy didn't just have his headlights on, he had his high beams on!! I backed away from the water and start to signal the driver to kill the lights—he gave no response. Then the guy pulls right up lights blazing and he staggers out of his Jeep. I politely ask him to kill his lights. "Turn the f****** lights off!!!" (That is polite isn't it?) The guy was the epitome of "privileged Hampton summer native." This guy was wearing his Topsiders, Ralph Lauren shorts, polo shirt and was totally drunk.

"Hey, how's it going? Catch anything? I needed some air you know, party. Catch anything? Hey I've fished here before, got a rod in the Jeep somewhere what are you using? Any fish here?" I roll my eyes and think that if I ignore this guy he'll leave. No such luck! He dug around the back of his Jeep and came out with a two-piece rod which he hastily slapped together and headed for the rocks. "Loaded" and loaded for bear, he almost fell over when casting his bucktail out into the water. I was thinking, "No pork trailer, hmmm, okay, he'll get bored or he'll fall in, either way I'll be able to get back to fishing."

"I got something!" He yelled. "Sure he does," I thought, "he has to have hung up on the bottom, he'll break his line and he'll leave." This is when moderate bad went to serious bad! I hear his drag screaming. Shit, this goog really does have something. Okay, I'm really not a bad guy so I put down my rod and go see if I can help him out. "Keep the tip up. Let the rod do the work. Don't give him any slack." After several minutes of my expert advice and encouragement the fish is now near the rocks. "Hang on. You are going to kill yourself on those rocks." I yell. I mean the guy could barely stand up and now he's heading out onto the rocks in topsiders. "Just keep the rod tip up, the line tight, stop reeling and I'll land the fish for you." I turned on my neck lamp and worked my way to the edge of the rocks.

"Damn!!" The fish was large, easily 40 pounds! I was sleep-deprived, hot, and had been beating the water for an hour, suddenly this drunk shows up, takes one cast and hooks a 40?!

The goog must have heard me mumbling. Excited, he takes a step closer and starts to slip. Again I hold him to save him. I reach down and I grab the fish by the lip, slide it out and hand it over to the surprised drunk. He looks at it and smiles; he is suddenly in "Fish Heaven!" He slurs a "Thanks a million buddy" and he staggers back to his Jeep, throws the fish in and then finally leaves. I'm too bummed out at this point to fish any more and pack it in and head home.

A week later I read a report in *The Fisherman Magazine*. Forty-two-pound bass caught blah, blah, blah… I knew it was the goog's fish. That's when it hit me; that drunken nitwit had caught the kind of fish that maybe comes along once every few years, a fish that surfcasters long for.

You want to know what really sticks in my craw all these years later: Wondering if I could have gotten away with gaffing the goog instead of the fish!

THE NEW BROWN'S

By Frank Blasko

The Brown's is a boulder-strewn stretch on Montauk Point's southside, which begins at the west end of Turtle Cove, stretches around the bottom of Camp Hero and ends at the Sewer Pipe. –D.J.M.

There is a new stretch of south side beach which has recently been reshaped and aptly named "The New Brown's." Let me explain how this happened. If you are thinking it is due to a recent heave you are only *partially* correct—allow me to explain.

We all have our vices. I have given up just about all of them (I got tired of going to jail) except for food and pitch-black, bitter iced coffee. Now as food is one of my last few vices, from time to time I over indulge. Coffee you can drop into that same category. In the case of this night both were true. After a sizable meal of sushi, I made the 1 1/2 hour ride to Montauk to skish the last of the flood tide. *(Note: Skishing is the practice of donning a wetsuit and your regular surfcasting gear and swimming out off of the beach a few hundred yards and drifting the currents as you fish for stripers).* Along the way, I had a nice refreshing 22-ounce iced coffee from Dunkin Donuts. This was gone before Watermill and I thought a cold diet Pepsi would complement things quite nicely.

Upon arriving at Montauk, my friend and I observed a considerable yet acceptable swell. The hardest part of skishing is getting out past the white water without getting destroyed. In order to accomplish this, one must lie on ones back and kick head first into the surf. The consequences of this are the occasional and unexpected mouths full of sea water. Due to the high surf, it was more than a mouth full…or five. (This is where the heave contributes to The "New Brown's.") Not to worry though, once you are past the wash it is just a matter of being gently lulled up and down by the constant rollers with an occasional over the head wave. Now I'm no scientist, but I think the recipe here could have a lot to do with how the beach changed that night.

Take one large 235-pound man, fill him with sushi, iced coffee, diet Pepsi, copious amounts of sea water and a hint of sand, have that same large man physically exert him self continuously for 20 minutes, then shake the large man up and down in rough seas until his "little" stomach begins to gurgle.

At this point we had completed our drift with no fish to show for our efforts so we decided to head back into the cove. Getting in can be as rough as getting out except you try to pick a landing area which is sand beach rather than rocky shoreline (good luck in the pitch black!). So while swimming in you add a touch more sea water to an already gurgling stomach and you have a recipe for... well stay tuned.

Now here is the key: if your wetsuit fits right it will be snug, snug induces significant stomach cramping to the uneasy stomach. If you do have a good, snug 5- or 7-millimeter suit, you will quickly add full cramping and colon spasms to your already unnerving sick stomach. If you do not have these qualities, you are doing the whole thing wrong.

Upon landing, I was faced with a race against wet neoprene. This is a fabulous sight, like watching a NASCAR driver on fire after a crash. Fortunately I was rather tired from the ordeal and my fatigue level gave my stomach a nice head start. By the time I reached the bluff area, there was no longer any option other than to do what I had to do, squat on the sand.

Being somewhat of a resourceful individual, I carry with me a handy knife. Another thing I do, which has come into question on more than one occasion is wear underwear beneath my wetsuit. This is an arguable debate amongst wetsuiters. The benefits here are twofold: one, it prevents a rash; two when coupled with the handy knife, you have yourself some useful rags and right when and where you need them most.

After a satisfactory disposal and a quick sea rinse, which was supplemented by a huge feeling of relief, I suited back up (this time, with only the left leg of my boxers intact) and back in business. Being something of an animal, and I will let you all decide how much of an animal, I felt that I had marked my territory. But as if that wasn't enough, I felt the best way to do this would be to place a dead eel atop the newly formed sand pile along the bluff. My territory was forever marked, well at least until the next tide rolled in.

So, next time you are rounding the bend at Turtle Cove, keep your eyes open for a small, inconspicuous structure. If you find it, you have reached the area now known as "The New Browns."

A HALLOWEEN STORY

By Bill Lellis

Have you ever had something happen to you that you've never told anyone about simply because no one would believe you anyway and you don't want to spend the time deflecting ridicule? One of those things that as the details fade with time you even begin to question your own recollections and perceptions of the event? This is one of those stories.

The fact that it happened on Halloween night doesn't help. Now I'm not superstitious and Halloween to me is no different than any other day of the year. If I fished every day then the likelihood of a particular incident happening on a particular day like Halloween would be 1:365. That's a statistical fact. But I don't fish every day, more like 20, and if Halloween happens to be one of those days then the chance of an incident happening on Halloween is just that much greater. But still, the fact that it happened on Halloween night doesn't help my credibility.

The incident happened in the late 1980's or perhaps early 1990's. High tide was about midnight at Montauk and I wanted to fish the last two hours of incoming under the lighthouse. The wind was strong out of the northeast and gannets had shown up on the east end a few days earlier, hopefully signaling the arrival of herring with big bass in tow.

I stopped at Johnny's Tackle earlier that afternoon and picked up a new blue darter, although in the back of my head I knew it would probably be too windy to throw. Still, it's my go-to plug in late-fall under the candle and I wanted it in my bag. I arrived at the lighthouse around 8:30 or 9:00 p.m. and secured a spot on my favorite rock. I was expecting the place to be packed for a midnight flood in late October but I found myself strangely alone. Maybe there was a bite someplace else that everyone but me knew about? Or maybe everyone stayed home to trick-or-treat with the kids? Either way, I found the solitude odd.

Conditions looked great. The night was black save the periodic flash of the beam as it swept high above my head. The wind was blowing hard in my face and the howl in my ears muffled the moan of lighthouse fog horn. The sea was a chaotic mix of waves smacking against the rocks, first from the right, then from the left. An eerie blend of fog, foam, and spray hung in the air and covered my glasses, reducing visibility to nil. I licked the spray from my lenses several times in the first few minutes; a trick I had learned over many years of casting to maintain some semblance of visibility, but tonight there was no hope, the mist was just too heavy.

Working a plug was going to be tough. The current was pulling strong right to left against wind and a large bucktail was likely the only thing I would be able to both cast and stay in contact with in this sweep. Still, that new darter was burning a hole in my bag and I needed at least one cast to convince myself it couldn't work in these conditions.

My first cast was not particularly strong and by the time I gathered the slack the plug had been tossed into the rocks below me and hung up right at the water line. Crap. That was stupid. I licked my glasses again and studied the pattern and strength of the incoming waves. If it was an older plug, I would have broken it off and tried retrieving it the following morning, but this was my first cast and I couldn't let it go that easily.

I made it to the rock without incident and freed the plug with relative ease. As I stood up to begin my retreat I noticed the sea suddenly seemed empty in front of me. Like a black hole forming in the water with an accompanying sucking sound. I'd seen this before once or twice and it's not a welcome sight. It's the prelude to the arrival of Three Sisters and panic filled my brain. For those of you not familiar to the term, "Three Sisters" refers to a series of three successive waves that sometimes form during large storm events which are of greater magnitude and intensity than the other waves. Each sister is usually more evil than its immediate predecessor.

The first sister buckled my knees. I never saw the second. She came down cold and black out of the night and drove me backwards into the rocks. I landed upside down in a crevice, shattering my rod during the fall. The third sister dropped what seemed like a ton of water on my chest, knocking the wind out of me and pushing me further into the boulders.

I'm not sure how long I was unconscious, but when I awoke I found myself lying on my back, shivering violently and in extreme pain. The tide had come in and I was completely submerged, save my face and right foot, which was wedged between two rocks above my head. The broken rod was jammed in my back, and I wasn't sure if it had penetrated my chest cavity or if I had broken some ribs during the fall. Either way, I was having great difficulty breathing. I struggled for what seemed like an eternity to free myself, but exhaustion eventually won out and I surrendered to my fate. I thought of my wife and two daughters. I thought of my family and friends. Childhood memories of fluke fishing in my grandfather's wooden skiff on Shinnecock Bay floated through my head like an old home movie. The shivering stopped and I didn't feel cold anymore. In fact, I started to feel strangely at peace with the world.

My thoughts were suddenly interrupted by a voice coming through the night and the pain and panic returned. "Hold on buddy, hold on, I'm coming!" I felt someone unlacing my wading boot and pulling my foot from the rock. "You're alright, buddy, you're alright. I gottcha now." The stranger grabbed my left arm and pulled me to my feet. "Good thing your light was still on or I would never have seen you down here." He helped me to the safety of the upper rocks and I sat for a moment, disoriented and shaken.

"Hank," he said and extended his hand for a customary shake. I felt nothing. I licked my glasses and peered into the darkness at the man. He was a large guy, maybe 60-ish with a shadow of an unshaven beard. He was wearing an old set of rubberized waders and a torn yellow raincoat. In his left hand he clenched a heavy fiberglass rod with wire guides that had surely seen a thousand or more battles. Attached was a beaten reel like I haven't seen for years, maybe a Crack or old Garcia-Mitchell strung with thick monofilament. "You gotta be careful down there buddy. You shouldn't be fishing alone on a night like tonight." I thanked him profusely as he studied my face. "Wait, don't I know you?" he asked, studying me even more intently. "Didn't you used to fish out here a lot in the late 60's or early 70's; at night, by yourself?" "Yes," I replied. "I recognize you," he said. "Not many guys out here with your physique." He turned towards the water, cupped his hands to his mouth and screamed out, "Hey Joe, look who's here, it's the Bean-Pole!"

I could barely make out the guy Hank was talking to. A shadowy figure in the fog perched maybe 10 rocks left of where I had been fishing. Must have come down while I was stuck. He was hard into a fish and he seemed perilously close to losing his balance. As he turned his head to address Hank, the fish suddenly surged and I swear I saw the guy plunge face-first into the wash. But when I jumped to my feet to help, he was still standing strong squared up to the ocean. "I keep telling him he sets his drag too tight." Hank mused. "One day he's going to get pulled right off his rock, but he never listens."

It was then I saw another smaller figure below us. It appeared to be a young boy, scrambling along the jetty, searching frantically for something among the rocks. He was gaunt and wild looking, with a hollow gaze that he frequently shot off in the distance behind us. "That kid shouldn't be down there" I said to Hank. "That's Nicky. Mike's boy. His dad went back to the car to change reels and told Nicky not to touch his stuff while he was gone. But Nicky don't listen to nobody and now and he's lost his Dad's favorite yellow darter. Mike's gonna kill him when he gets back." Water washed over the strange apparition and he faded in and out of the darkness. "Some kids gotta learn the hard way," sighed Hank.

"Dat's for sure!" a voice boomed from over my right shoulder. I spun around to find a large dark-haired guy sitting right behind me. He was dressed in street clothes, not looking much like a fisherman, and he cradled a large hero in his lap. His general appearance and oblivion to the weather seemed strangely out of place. He extended a huge open hand in my direction, but before I could accept his shake, he gasped, clutched his chest, and started to slide off the rock towards the ocean. I lunged to intercept his fall, but he wasn't there. I looked up and he still sat comfortably on the rock. "I'm seeing things," I thought, just as Hank proclaimed to no one in particular "I told Sal all them cold cuts was no good for his heart, but does he listen? Nah. Not his fault. He's Italian. In his blood I guess." Sal shrugged his shoulders and grinned widely.

I could now make out a new figure against the surf. A tall skinny guy perched on the rock I had just been washed off. He seemed to be fumbling with a plug just as a large wave crushed down on him and he disappeared into the night. To the left Joe was being yanked into the ocean once again and Nicky faded in and out of the rocks. I jumped up and watched the scene repeat itself over and over. Guy fumbling, wave pounding, guy fumbling, wave pounding. "My God," I thought, "that's me!"

"Welcome to the real Montauk Point Surf Club Billy-Boy!" bellowed Hank. "We've been waiting a long time for a new member." Sal laughed so hard it triggered another heart attack which sent him sliding back down the rocks to the absolute delight of Nicky, who leaped wildly flailing his arms in the air. The whole scene spun madly around my head, until the wind and the spray, the laughter and the jeers, the rocks and the sea all melded together and I could no longer make sense of the scene I was witnessing. Blackness ensued.

I woke with a start. Dawn had broken to a gray and windy Montauk morning. I was curled up in the back of my Subaru in the lower lot, soaking wet and shivering violently. I was still dressed in my waders and my left ribs and right ankle burned with pain. I unfolded myself and opened the car door. On the ground lay the handle end of my broken rod. The reel was mangled beyond repair and the contents of my surf bag were scattered across the parking lot. "Oh God," I thought as I limped my way across the pavement, "bad dream." I spent most of the morning lying on the floor of the men's rest room trying to warm up and gather myself. Around noon I returned to the lighthouse to retrieve my lost boot, which I found still wedged between the rocks by the water line. The heel was wrapped in a ball of worn monofilament, to which was attached the remains of an old wooden plug. The hooks and hardware had rusted away and the paint had long since peeled, save one very small chip remaining in the crease of the lip, revealing its original color. It was a darter. It had once been yellow.

Lot's of guys use yellow darters under the Montauk Lighthouse, and I'm sure the rocks claim untold hundreds every year. Just like a nightmare on Halloween night, I place no particular significance to the fact that I found that plug wedged in behind my boot on the day I almost drowned in the Montauk surf. But I keep that plug in my bag and carry it with me whenever I fish, just in case on one night, in the fog and the black and the blinding spray, on a night when the Three Sisters come calling, I meet up again with the hollow eyed boy with the lost gaze and the lost soul, so I can return that plug to its rightful owner, and send him on his journey.

SWEPT AWAY

By Larry Welcome

The bite had been good for the last few trips and the season was running out fast, in our neck of the woods...the season ends quickly.

Probably because of this we made a few decisions with a little more haste than we should have. We tend to take chances that most fishermen wouldn't risk anyway, but this time we may have gotten a little carried away. We got to our spot and looked it over and said as a group, "Whoa now, is this a good idea?" The wind was out of the northwest at about 25 to 30 mph and there was a good ground swell working in with the wind; that combined with the powerful east-southeast current told us to maybe re-think what we were about to do.

The wind and sea conditions were bad but there was also a lunar high tide—these factors were coming together to form the perfect storm of stupidity and we were steering right into the eye. What's the next move you ask? Well, let's go out on the bar two hours down in the tide instead of three hours down like we would normally do under ideal conditions. Remember, the season is winding down and who knows how many more trips we had left in the year? Let's get as much out of what's left of this year as possible, let's go out there now!

Now, you have to understand that this is a dangerous place to fish on a calm night and it's a big risk on a rough night. But, on a night like this one... it's just plain stupid. We went anyway.

I'm 6-foot, 6-inches tall and weigh about 250 pounds so it takes a lot to move me when I dig in, but Kip was with me on this night and he's just 5-foot, 9 and weighs in at a solid 150. Rob was also there and he fell just about in the middle of Kip and me in both height and weight. We've all made this trip many times and under all sorts of conditions and we usually have good luck so we were confident and we just headed out there.

The walk is about 600 yards out into the water on a bar to a rock pile and takes about 20 minutes on a normal night taking baby steps all the way due to an 8-knot cross-current that tries to drive you into the deep with every step. Well, we were about 150-yards into the crossing when Kip said that his surf bag was "parachuting" and dragging him sideways so I took it from him and put it on my shoulder and we continued on. Another 200 yards and Kip went sailing past me, the current was driving him through the 2- to 3-foot surges which were adding to his dilemma, so I grabbed his rod and pulled him back uptide to my left and kept him there with my left arm each time he was lifted by a wave and we kept going.

At this point we really couldn't go back because we were going with the current and it would have been impossible for Kip to go back against the waves and current, so we forged on. We were about 50 yards from the rock pile and we entered an eddy that reduced the current by about half and gave us a little rest. We were feeling like we had made it when Kip suddenly went flying past me again on top of a wave and behind me. I was able to grab his rod tip again and hold on but Kip could not get his feet down, in fact they were riding on the surface and just flailing in the current. We were in trouble now and Kip said, "Larry, let me go, there's no sense in us both going and I'm already gone." At that point Rob had the tip of my rod and we were a daisy chain of idiots all about to go into the deep.

I've fished with these two guys for years in all kinds of water and we've been thrown around, dunked, frozen, bashed into rocks and all the other stuff that makes surf fishing so much fun. We've always come through it safely, with good memories and usually a couple of good fish—this night was looking like it might go a bit differently. After all those years we fished together I realized at this very moment that I didn't know whether or not Kip could swim or how he might react being out in the deep by himself. I've seen people panic when they were in trouble in the water and I didn't know if Kip would panic! So, even though I could have gotten to the safety of the rock pile with Rob I made the decision to go with

Kip. I told Rob to let go of my rod and let me go. There's no sense in all three of us going and someone needs to get back and make a call.

So off we go and in about three minutes we were about 500 yards offshore and moving fast. In the first few seconds we had the good sense to drop all our gear; two custom rods with VS250s, two Surfcaster surfbags loaded with all our favorites, two belts with Boga Grips, pliers and knives, our Korkers and boots...all tolled about $4000 worth of gear in 15 seconds lost to the deep.

We've heard many stories over the years about how dangerous this spot can be and what would happen if you were swept away. When you're being carried by the current, all this immediately comes into your head so I made my way over to Kip so we could keep each other company on the ride and sort of boost each others morale while we decided what to do and how to do it. Well it turns out that as the water gets deeper the current slows a little and then a little deeper and it slows a little more until at about 800 yards out we were able to start inching our way more south and less east and then some west and less south and then west and some north. All this time (about 45 minutes to an hour) Rob was fighting to get back to the shore to call for help and finally, a fisherman on the shore realized what was going on and made the call. But by now we were making our way west and north and we were about maybe 200 yards out when the fire department showed up with a Zodiac inflatable and they were not about to be denied a good rescue so they launched, came out to get us and all ended well.

A few days later I went back with mask, snorkel and fins to look for out gear, I was able to find Kip's rod and reel and belt with all the components attached, but all of my gear was gone forever. It has all been replaced now and I am alive to tell my story.

THE NEWBIE AND BIG MOMMA

By Pete Burawa

Today was one of those days that will stand out with the worst of them. I would rather have been skunked than to go through what I just went through. So far the fall had been crazy, especially considering everything that was going on at my house! My wife finally got a Saturday off and we had made plans, first we would visit her mom in orthopedic rehab and then take a nice drive east to catch sunset and do some fishing.

Well everything was going along fine; we even got a bottle of wine to drink while we waited out the tide. I put two bait rods out just for kicks and we were enjoying the day. As we were hanging out a guy with a tackle box came along and stopped to talk. I spied his 12-inch steel leader connected to a blue pencil popper. I commented about the need for a long mono leader if he was going to fish the nearby jetty, then I helped him out and rigged him up right.

While we were talking I saw him check out the three Van Staals on custom built rods and the whole soup-to-nuts rig he seemed impressed and offered lots of compliments and gratitude. After a while, we said our good-byes and he went on down the beach. After an hour or so, I pulled in the bait rods with the intention of plugging the hole a little ways down the beach where I could see a few buggies were parked so we got into the truck and headed down.

As I pulled up I saw my 'new friend' was into a fish. So is this large woman in sneakers who yells at me not to stop. I'm smiling ear-to-ear thinking, "Jeez this should be easy." I get out and cast a tin out to the bar, nothing. I throw again nothing! I grab the other the rod with the blue pencil and I'm working the water to a froth and still, nothing! Newbie and Big Momma are now into their fourth fish since I stopped. Momma is squealing with delight as her drag is buzzing and she can't budge this fish with her small yellow rod. Finally, she ends up landing a respectable 20-pound bass. Newbie lands his first keeper as I confirm the length against the mark on my rod. Me? Still nada, nothing, zilch!!

Now I am starting to lose it when I figure that I should get the wife involved. She hasn't cast a rod since B.C. (before children) to make it easier, I cast for her. She starts a retrieve, *bingo*, a bluefish! While I'm unhooking that bluefish, the bass are slurping down peanuts at my feet. I cast again.... nothing, nothing, nothing. It's like my hooks had a whammy put on them by a gypsy.

Then I finally hook up, a bluefish, yuck and small at that. I cast again, but I sense a wind knot in my fingers as I retrieve. I pause to pull it out, my wife then figures that it would be a good time to cast while I'm busy. She casts and I see her hand searching for the line to put onto the roller as a large loop of braided line comes flying across my face from her reel. The line proceeds to tangle on my plug bag, pliers and everything else in the way. Wind knots on wind knots on two different rods. My temperature was rising.

I started to get a handle on this while I watch Newbie and Big Momma land two more fish, this time in the mid-20's. Meanwhile the line is streaming down the beach and all I'm thinking is, "let's get as much of this stuff back on the reel and then we'll fish with the backup rod." Finally I get both outfits under control. One has a knot that would require a vascular surgeon to figure out. I give up and just crank it in. The other rod comes out ok. At this point I'm really frustrated and Newbie comes up and asks me if he can keep his fish in my cooler. I don't know what I said, but it wasn't yes.

I hook a couple of bluefish as do Newbie and Momma.

My wife retreats to the truck, and then informs me its time to go home. I tried to explain to her, "There is a blitz going on, I missed most of it untying the tangle from your cast and unhooking the poor bluefish that were confused enough to hit our plugs and now we have to go home?"

I just needed some time to salvage what was left of my fishing prowess. I had to redeem myself in front of Newbie and Big Momma. I just couldn't leave now. Of course she wouldn't understand all that stuff. I knew she wouldn't understand because of what she said next: "You weren't catching anything anyway."

If there was Viagra for fishing, I needed it now. My fishing libido turned my 11-foot Lami into a 2-foot Snoopy rod. 1100 milligrams please! I think I can, I think I can. I started off to the surf line and out of the corner of my eye I caught the body language, arms folded across her chest, looking away, top lip quivering ready to explode into a thousand expletives about me and my stupid hobbies. If I argue with her here…well?

I began to take a cast, then realized that the price would be exorbitant, way out of contention, I turned around and racked the rods.

The silent routine was about to begin. I aired up in silence, drove home in silence, and ate dinner in silence. But let it be known, I was going to be out at 3:00 a.m. and you can bet my wife would not be with me and I hoped to God that Big Momma and Newbie wouldn't be there either!

A BLITZ AT TURTLE COVE

By Mike "Saltheart" White

For many years in the late 80's and early 90's, I would fish at Montauk Point with my friends Chris and Gardner. Gardner was Chris' stepfather and was almost 70 years old. We were in our 30's. Gardner had a nice motor home and he and Chris would drive out to Montauk from New Jersey and I would take the ferry from New London to Orient Point and then either drive around to Montauk or ride the ferries to and from Shelter Island to the Hamptons and drive in from there. If it was in the summer we would camp at Hither Hills Campground and in the fall we were allowed to park in the lower parking lot right there near Montauk Light since our vehicle was completely self contained (there were no tents or sleeping in your car allowed and the rangers were very diligent with enforcement).

We would fish early morning before dawn, and sometimes all night. I had good success along the shore north of the light using rigged eels. We never fished under the light due to the crowds. We were not into that kind of crowded fishing scene. These were the days when the size limit on stripers was 36 inches. I always did well there, especially Thanksgiving weekend. It was cold at that time of course so having the heated motor home was really living in luxury for fishermen.

One of the funny things I remember was Mr. Ketchup Head. Mr. Ketchup Head was an alarm clock that was the shape and size of a big Heinz ketchup bottle. This obnoxious little fellow would wake us up in the middle of the night so we could catch the desired tides. When the alarm went off, Mr. Ketchup Head would start in a really loud voice, "Its time to get up, get up right away, if you don't get up now, you'll have to Ketchup all day!" After this beckoning a couple of times, he would then sound all kinds of beeping honking alarm sounds similar to the beeping and honking sirens the ambulances and fire trucks used.

On one trip in late-August we were there and during the day we decided to go scout out Turtle Cove which is a small cove south of the light. It is nicely protected from the wind and there is a small beach there. Well as we walked down the path to the cove, a huge blitz of bluefish erupted in the cove.

We ran back to get our rods and started casting to the fish. We hooked up almost every cast and before long had a few blues each stacked up on the shore. Chris had a smoker and made delicious smoked bluefish in it so we were saving the fish. There were a lot of people on the beach that day and one funny thing that happened was these older women in some kind of ethnic type dresses, started stealing bluefish from our pile. I guess they also wanted some to eat and since we were catching all we wanted, we let them take some fish.

After about 45 minutes, we had plenty of fish and were leaning on the poles for a little rest. A kid that looked to be about 10 years old walked up to me and very politely asked if he could use my pole to try to catch a fish. I said, "sure" and gave him the pole. Now this was a 12-foot rod with a big Penn 850SS reel on it. He had trouble handling it and couldn't get the lure out to the fish so I cast it into the fish and he then dragged it through and hooked up. He landed the fish and very politely said thank you and offered the pole back to me. I said go ahead catch another but he said, "Nah, there are people waiting."

I turn around and now there is a bunch of kids, all waiting in a line for a turn at catching a fish. Chris and I looked at each other and had a big laugh then started taking the kids one by one and giving them a turn at catching a blue. It was the best thing to see the excitement on their faces as they hooked up. Each kid was perfectly behaved and with no arguing handed the pole to the next kid in line after they had their turn. Pretty soon the kids in the line are getting bigger. There was a kid about 14 and a kid about 16 in line now, so we just kept on helping them catch fish with our poles.

I then turn around for the next "kid" and there is a beautiful girl, maybe 23 years old in a tiny bikini that looked like it was made from 3 Band-Aids. She asks if she could try for a fish. I said sure and cast it out for her. She hooks a fish and she lights up all excited trying to reel it in but being a very small lady she is having trouble handling the 12-foot pole. So she asks, "What's the best way to do this?" I felt awfully embarrassed telling her to put the butt between her legs, but of course, that IS the best way to do it. So she puts the butt end between her legs and lands the fish. There are no more kids in line so she caught a couple more then she was tired.

So then I turned around and there is a grown woman, fully dressed waiting. So I hand her the rod but she says no, she doesn't want to try it but her husband, about 30 years old, who is from Oklahoma and never saw the ocean until that day, wants to try for a fish but he's too embarrassed to ask so she is asking for him. I waved him over and handed him the pole and he cast it out by himself and he hooked up. You could see by the look on his face when he hooked up that this was the most exciting thing he had experienced in a while. He got a couple of fish and then the fish moved out away from shore and eventually off to the south. So ended The Turtle Cove Blitz and one of the most entertaining afternoons I ever had fishing.

"MY FIRST 40"

By Edward Greenberg

(The following story takes place on 3 consecutive nights dating from July 29 through August 1, 1989. The new moon was on August 1.)

I had spent a good deal of the summer of 1988 learning to bucktail Shinnecock Inlet's east jetty by observing an old timer, by the name of Walter. Walter knew every inch of the inlet like the back of his hand. He fished only with bucktails and he CAUGHT! For weeks on end, the most I got out of Walter was a grunted "Mornin'." This did not deter me in my quest to figure out his "secret formula" for bucktailing the inlet.

One morning, about a week after Labor Day, Walter arrives just as the eastern sky is getting lighter. I say my usual "Good morning" and get no reply. He gears up, and to my surprise, comes up to me and says, "Kid, if you ain't losin' 'em, you ain't fishin' 'em right." He saw the look of confusion on my face, so in as few words as possible, he explained how close to the bottom I needed to fish and how this would result in lots of lost bucktails. Now I understood! I started to hang up bucktails but I also began to get the feel for the bottom and began to catch fish!

By the 1989 season, after much hard work and practice I had it down fairly well. At that time, the east jetty was in pretty rough shape (it was completely rebuilt in the fall of 1992, so the spots of which I speak no longer exist). The south end (ocean side) of the jetty was a tumbled down collection of rocks that we locals called "The Jungle." On a good night you could access it only after several hours of falling water. If there was a moderate swell on any particular night you took your life in your hands but you had to get to the spot in order to get the correct angle on the hole that was your target at the time.

The First Night. 7/29-7/30

I arrived around 10 p.m. Low water was around 11:30 but didn't actually slack for another 2 ½ hours. It was a quiet night without much of a swell. I made my way out to The Jungle without a whole lot of expectation, after all it was almost August, a time nicknamed by surfcasters as the "summer doldrums." No one else was on the jetty that night but I did see a flash light on the beach in front of where, the then campsites were. As soon as the bucktail rolled off the shoal and dropped into the hole, it got smacked. The bite was hot and I totaled 22 bass from 12 to 16 pounds before the tide finally died. I was psyched!

The Second Night: 7/30-7/31

I arrived around 10 p.m. I should have been an hour later, but remember, I was psyched! I found the swell up a bit so the place I had to get to was inaccessible. I could not get to the spot for at least another hour or so. As the time drew near I noticed a light on the jetty out in front of me, I didn't expect that, bummer! I geared up and started out. I came upon two guys fishing a safe dry spot right before The Jungle. "Any luck?" I asked. "No, not yet but last night we saw a light go on and off a lot out here while we were fishing the beach so we thought we would give it a shot tonight."

A little more small talk then I continued to work my way a little deeper into the Jungle. "Watch yourself it doesn't look too safe out there," one of the fellows yelled to me. "I'll be very careful." I found a decent rock and made a few casts but I was not getting to the right spot on the shoal. As the tide dropped I worked my way out to the rock that I had fished the night before. Ten minutes after getting to my perch I was into the first fish of the night. It felt like a much better fish than any of the ones that I had yesterday. After a good battle I finally slid the fish up between two rocks and to my feet. I was right, the fish weighed 22 pounds on my Manley handheld scale. I totaled 14 stripers before the end of the tide all between 20 and 27 pounds. (If I remember correctly the two guys had one small bluefish between them.)

The Third Night: 7/31-8/1

On the third night of this particular pattern I arrived again around 10 p.m. this time I was *really* psyched! The wind was up from the south-southeast, as was the swell and the number of fishermen. There was no way I was getting to my spot with the water this high. (My time management skills have gotten much better now that I'm older.) Once I got suited up I made my way out onto the rocks. After a short conversation on my way out I knew that "some guy was banging big fish here all night last night. The guys in the camper next to ours swear it is true," said one of the guys.

I fished another spot on the jetty for zero while keeping an eye on the tide and the other guys. Finally I said "to hell with it" and headed out to The Jungle. I worked my way to my rock. I had to time the incoming swells in order to get past the two really low spots as to not get washed off the jetty. I got settled into my spot and began to cast but quickly realized that with the wind, I wasn't quite reaching where I needed my bucktail to be. As the tide dropped some more, I was eventually able to get a few more yards out into the Jungle and with a little drop back (letting another 15- to 20-yards of line "drop back" into the current before I picked it up and put it on the roller), I was able to feel the bucktail roll into the hole. Bang! I was in. The first fish went 32-pounds on the Manley. By the time I released it I found that two brave souls had ventured out to join me. In the next hour or so, I took six more fish between 23 and 34 pounds. I was very wet and very happy and I was losing the tide.

Hey I wasn't complaining it had been a pretty darn good session. Five more casts and I'm out of here, I thought to myself. I cast again and bang again, another fish had taken the bucktail. This fish also felt decent, about what the mid-20's had felt like, not being terribly experienced I failed to realize that there was much less current now as the had tide slowed considerably. I got the fish close to the jetty and put my light on so as to steer the fish around a rock and to my feet. It was at this point that two things happened that I did not expect; one was I saw a fish it was much larger than any fish that I had caught previously; secondly when the fish saw the light it took off. It almost pulled me off my rock as the drag screamed.

That loud, high pitched, clicking from the drag of my old Crack 300 got the attention of the two guys that were fishing nearby. By the time I stopped the run one of the guys had worked his way a little closer and offered to help. "No. I'm good," I assured him.

Ten minutes later, I had the fish back to rocks in front of me along with the undivided attention of several other guys on the jetty. My light was on as I tried to navigate the fish between a couple rocks to where I could grab it but the tide had slacked and I couldn't get it close enough. No worry I was prepared. I got my little hand gaff out (remember it was 1989 and I had never even heard of a Boga grip) and I timed the swell and then quickly got down low on the rock in order to carefully lip gaff the fish. I gaffed the fish as planned and I lifted it, or should I say tried to lift it but when I did my foot began to slip and I lost all my leverage.

At this point, I couldn't move and a wave hit the rocks and completely soaked me. There I was rod in one hand, little gaff in the other, soaked and losing my footing. "You need a hand?" There came a voice once again from out of the night. In no uncertain terms I exclaimed, "Yes!" I think if I had been alone, I may have got myself into trouble as I would have gone off the jetty before I let go of that fish. Lucky for me it never came down to me having to make that decision.

The great fish went 45 ½ pounds on my scale and with my new best fishing buddy having a good grip on my wader belt and with the waves continually pounding me, I swam that girl for a good five minutes as I tried to revive her. It was a feeling I will never forget; the strength of her tail kick as she swam out of my hands and back to her home.

My first 40 was a memory I will never forget.

Years later, I finally got around to asking Walter why it took him so long to talk to me. I got the quintessential Walter answer; "Wanted to be sure you were serious 'bout fishin'."

THE FOG

By Bill Lellis

If you spend enough time with a group of surfcasters who have been at the game for a while, the conversation will at some point invariably turn to stories of odd and often unsettling occurrences experienced while fishing. These experiences have usually occurred late at night. Often while fishing alone. Stories of UFOs. Stories of sea monsters. Apparitions. Unfamiliar sounds or voices. Figures that appear or disappear in the dark without explanation. People or animals oddly out of place for the circumstances. These are stories not meant for large and unfamiliar audiences, but rather small circles of trusted friends, generally told with a tinge of hesitation for fear of ridicule, but offered up with the vague hope that someone else had a similar experience to help calm lingering doubts of ones senses and sensibilities. This is my story.

I was fishing Montauk around the full moon in July a few years back. There was talk going around of large bass on bunker on the south side, so I decided to spend the full night searching them out. I parked in the lower lot of the Lighthouse, walked to the Sewer Pipe, and started fishing just before sunset. The tide was approaching high, the air heavy, and the moon rising as I picked my way west. My strategy for the evening was to walk and watch, best three casts in any one spot and move on. I reached Caswell's without a hit and passed by the last three casters I would see the rest of the night. I had a few rises and picked a few small fish over the next several points, but I eventually reached the trailer park at Ditch without finding the bunker I was looking for and decided to turn back. The night was unusually hot and humid for July, and even though I was wearing only light waders and a tee shirt, the heat and the miles were starting to take their toll.

The tide had dropped out by the time I made it back to Driftwood, but I decided to take one last shot at the hole on the cove side of Kings before calling it a night. I pushed out to my normal platform, but the tide was unusually low and I could see better rocks in front of me. I waded out as deep as I dared and found a perch on a flat submerged rock in ankle-deep water. It was dead calm with absolutely no wave set. The sky was crystal clear with a blazing moon. A beautiful night to be alive.

I made a few casts to the corner of the point with a yellow darter, but the tide was dead and I could feel no movement, so I switched to a bucktail with no better results. I was contemplating my next move when I began to notice the horizon darkening, and within a few moments the stars and moon disappeared and I was engulfed in a thick, consuming fog. I stood momentarily stunned by the speed at which the fog had overtaken me, and decided to leave before I became disoriented and lost my sense of direction towards shore.

Just as I started to step off the rock, I picked up a faint humming sound drifting over the water. I paused for a moment and listened intently as it got closer. I could make out the faint but distinct sound of a small outboard motor. It sounded old, stuttering, and horribly inadequate to be out in the ocean at all, let alone on a foggy night. As the sound neared, I could vaguely make out a muffle of human voices. Too low and too distant to discern words, but with a definite sense of anxiety in their speech. I listened as they passed me once, turned around, then passed a second time.

I strained to hear their voices, which seemed neither male nor female, just low, trembling, desperate tones. I called out a warning and asked if they needed help. The voices stopped, as if they could hear me but also could not discern my words. On about the third pass I felt they were so close that I reached out my arm instinctively to fend off being hit. But the collision never came, and at that moment the moon started to break through haze, the sky cleared, and the fog passed as quickly as it had arrived. I spun to my left, then to my right. There was nothing. No boat, no people, nothing. Just me, once again standing alone at the edge of the ocean under a blazing moon and a crystal clear night sky.

I made my way back to shore, filling my waders as I stepped off that distant rock. I sat dazed on the sand, trying to come to grips with the events of the evening. Was it a dream? I hear of guys falling asleep while standing on rocks in the wee hours of the night. I didn't think so. Was it a hallucination, brought on by severe dehydration from the long walk and the heat? Probably not. I did drink two quarts of Gatorade along the way. A mirage? Sound has been known to travel long distances over the ocean. Possible, but that just changes the location of the event, not the event itself. Or had I, in fact, on that night by myself on the south side of Montauk Point, encountered some lost souls trapped in an endless fog, desperately trying to find safe harbor that will never come?

A ROUGH NIGHT ON THE ROCKS

By Kadir Akturk

It was a pitch black night in October of 2007. I took the long walk into one of my favorite spots on Montauk's southside, a place that doesn't get as much pressure as some of the other southside spots. It is a bit of walk but more often than not it's worth the trip.

Upon getting to my spot I began fishing. Down the shore I noticed a light from a head lamp, as far as I could tell there was just one other guy off in the distance. The water in front of me looked great! I was standing at one end of the cove with numerous rocks strewn about; the other guy is on the other end of the cove. The beauty of this spot is once you walk out about 30 or 40 yards, you are in some really turbulent water that gets deep fast.

I got up onto a rock and began casting my darter, my third cast resulted in a hook up, nothing big, a mid-teen sized fish. I continued to cast away picking up a similar-sized fish every fourth or fifth cast, a decent hit. The wind began picking up and I began to feel a chill through my wetsuit, the waves started to kick up and the surf began to build. The sets were coming in three's and four's at about 2- to 3-feet high. As the bite began to slow, I watched the other guy and noticed his light is going on and off (a sign of a fisherman catching and unhooking fish). Based on his success I decided to walk around the cove and fish the other side since it is the outgoing tide, I wanted to follow the fish.

I knew of a big, beautiful rock over in that area and I was hoping that he wasn't on it! It was a very good rock, one that you can't get to unless you are in wetsuit, and based on that I figured that I might have a decent shot at it. I finally got there and he was not on it, he was about 20 yards behind it and to the right. I was thinking he was in waders but I couldn't tell. Walking to this rock is tricky, there are small and medium size boulders all the way out, you have to negotiate every step you take. As you get closer to the boulder there is a hole around it. The depth goes from chest-deep to over your head and you still have at least 20 feet to go. It was at this point when I realize that the waves were bigger here, the depth is clearly visible as the drop off is much closer, just a stone's throw away. The wind was really driving hard into my face and I was really pumped! I finally got up on the rock after repeated efforts, the waves showing me no mercy, washing me off on occasion.

I began casting, throwing a bucktail straight into the wind, a dozen times without a touch. I began to lose faith in my bucktail so I reached into my bag for the 2-ounce Tattoo darter that got me the fish on the other side. The waves were coming in groups of three and four per set, but a little stronger and were bouncing off my stomach and thighs and pushing me back…I was confident though, the rock is large and I was holding fine with my Korkers. While changing my lure, I glanced up to check the waves and I saw one that was larger than the rest moving in. I felt a sense of panic as I could not get the lure onto the snap. I closed my bag and braced for impact, the wave crested over my head and took me with it toward the shore line.

Underwater now, my rod in my left hand, my plug with sharp treble hooks in my right hand, I was getting tossed like a garden salad! One after another, after another, the waves kept coming. I counted nine but I'm sure there were more, I tried "facing" them and diving through them but the weight of the Korkers on my feet and my heavy plug bag kept me almost vertical and the waves just plowed me over and turned me upside down. All the while I was struggling to hold onto my rod and plug.

At this point I was now at least 20 yards back from my perch and getting banged around pretty good. I spied a large egg-shaped rock and decided that I needed to work my way over to it. Man those waves are big and heavy when you are taking them in the face! Finally, I made it to the rock and put the plug into my left hand along with my rod and reached for the bubble weed on the rock with my right hand, I held on for dear life waiting for next batch of waves to roll over the rock and leave me a little time to catch my breath. All the while I begged the weeds not to disconnect from the rock.

I looked for the other guy and there was no sign of him, I thought the worst. The waves finally stopped their assault and the ocean suddenly fell calm. I looked at my rock now over 30 yards away and so was the shoreline. I decided that I needed to go back to shore to regroup. I worked my way out of the water, I was hurting. My right shoulder hurt and my shins and knees throbbed from the beating. I scanned the water and the beach to see if I could catch a glimpse of the other guy before I went looking for him. I saw a light come on, he was about 50 yards from where I saw him originally, he too was working his way in towards shore. He finally stumbles his way down to where I was sitting. "Wow, what the f*** was that?!!" We were both exhausted and just collapsed down onto the rocks still breathing heavily.

This was one of the few times I have actually felt helpless and really felt fear run through me. It wasn't adrenaline or excitement, not enjoyment, it was fear. As I reflected I thought that if I broke a leg or hit my head I might have been in seriously big trouble. Thank God I had a wetsuit on and not waders that night. The other guy was also in a wetsuit or he might have been in big trouble as well. After we calmed down, we both decided to walk out and leave well-enough alone....at least on this particular night. You don't get too many second chances.

HOOKED

By Thomas Oswald

Fish stories, we have all heard them, some of us have told them and others prefer to keep things to themselves. These tales, many of them tall, usually fall between "the one that got away" and the trophy on the wall. While the truth may be the first casualty in the creation of a good yarn, it is the true stories that do not get proudly told and retold that are often the most entertaining. Why, one might ask, would such events remain a mystery? Pull up a chair and listen.

As I made my way down the steep clay bluff on Montauk's fabled south side in the October darkness, I could barely see the large boulder some 50 feet offshore that would be my perch above the incoming tide for the next three hours. The annual striped bass migration was in full-swing and the anticipation of the first cast quickened my step.

A stiff breeze from the southeast brought the warm, briny air up the slope to greet me like an old friend. At the bottom, I slowly picked a path among the rounded stones in the now knee-deep water until I was atop my rock. The Big Dipper hung over my left shoulder and above the Milky Way spread its magic all the way to the horizon. Cast after cast I worked the water and the first hour passed without so much as a bump. Bucktails, metal-lip swimmers and needlefish were tossed with hopeful intensity as the speed of the current steadily increased while the tide rose slowly around me.

Now that the sea slid swiftly by from right to left, I decided it was time to employ the one plug that few in these parts would venture forth without: a yellow Super Strike Darter. Just the day before I had replaced its stock hooks with two, 4X strong hooks, a 4/0 on the front and a 3/0 in the rear, to achieve a little extra dig.

The lure bit into the current as it was swept along on a new moon tide and tracked an erratic path that mimicked a wounded baitfish. The rod tip throbbed and soon I felt the first bump of what was to be many. While the bass were on the small side, rats in the local jargon, I was heartened by their presence because I knew that this was a sign that bait had arrived and larger fish might soon follow.

Shortly, I was into a slightly larger fish in the 24-inch range. One of these turned out to be particularly frisky, thrashing about, not allowing me to grab its lip between my thumb and pointer finger. I decided the best method would be to pin the fish's body under my left armpit with just its head and gill plates sticking out. As I attempted to remove the lure's front set of treble hooks from the striper's mouth with my pliers, it squirted forward and upward as it shook its head vigorously from side to side. In an instant, the rear treble hook impaled my cheek just inches below my left eye. I froze in fear while the fish continued to thrash about in a manner that would have made a wild mustang proud. Eye to eye with that bass, I experienced for the first time what it felt like to be hooked.

Adrenaline pumped through my veins while the seriousness of my situation slowly became clear. I was in the dark, on a rock far from shore in 5-feet of water, alone with a crazed fish pinned to my face. Oh boy, not exactly the night I had envisioned. Then I thought about the darkness, no one around – thank goodness - how embarrassing. If it was daytime and I was on the next rock over, I would be asking myself who is that idiot with that fish hooked to his face?

Under the cover of darkness, I held the bass with my left hand tightly to my face as I felt blood run warmly down my neck. In my right hand was my precious setup – a $650, Van Staal spinning reel taped to a rare, $400, J. Kennedy Fisher rod. I held the rod between my knees as I attempted with both hands to remove the fish from the front hook while I was attached to the rear hook. With much effort, I managed to free the striper and release it back into the dark water below. I gingerly lowered myself into the waves and was soon back on shore, bloody and crestfallen.

Kneeling in the sand among the boulders, I felt my cheek and discovered that the hook had gone all the way in and the barb popped out about an inch over. I attempted blindly to cut the barb off the hook with the small pliers I carry but the cutters were too weak to cut the 4X strong hook. Resigning myself to the hour long ride to the emergency room in Southampton, I wearily began the climb back up the bluff.

Once at the top, I saw one other vehicle in the lot besides my own. A fellow surfcaster was at the tailgate of his truck preparing to fish the top of the tide. Sheepishly, I approached and asked him if he had a heavy-duty pair of pliers and if he could assist in solving my embarrassing dilemma. He looked at me and smiled and when he opened his mouth I immediately became alarmed. It was not what he said that concerned me but the strong odor of booze that wafted in my direction. An inebriated, novice surgeon operating on my face with a penlight in his mouth seemed at the time to be a risky proposition. I thought for a moment about that long ride to the hospital and the hungry stripers in the dark below. With one snip of the drunken stranger's pliers, I was released.

Not ten minutes later, I was back atop my rock, casting away. After all, I was hooked.

PART III

Rhode Island

THREE CASTS

By Gary Soldati

November 1988-Gary Soldati with 44 pound striper, it came on his third and last cast of the day.

It was 1988 and the run of the big November bass on Block Island was winding down, it had finally run it's course. Even though the number of big fish being caught on the island had dwindled, the number of fisherman had not. It was next to impossible to get a truck over on the Block Island Ferry! If you wanted to get onto the island you had to book well in advance. The years of the islanders having the bass all to themselves during this late-fall run were long gone.

There were beach buggies and trucks from New Jersey, New York, New Hampshire, Connecticut, Pennsylvania, Vermont, and my Massachusetts plates were just one set of many. Gone were the days of 12 casters on the bar at Southwest Point in a spot for six. The norm became throwing loaded needlefish into a stiff northeast wind where an errant cast would get you a punch in the mouth. Your reward for six hours of casting, if you could stand the cold, was maybe one hit. But there was always that chance that the hit would be a 50.

My buddy Rod and I were here to meet up with a seasoned crew from mainland Rhode Island. I met them by chance the year before when I had grown tired of reading all the fishing reports from Block and decided I needed to experience it for myself. I would be making a four night run to Block, sleeping in my truck. I was doing this blind, even though I had read numerous articles about Block Island I had never stepped foot on it until now.

I stopped into Covedge Tackle (long gone) to pick up a few things. I mentioned to the owner Henry Hetu that I was headed to Block. He said he was too and asked if I would give him a ride to the ferry. When we got off the ferry Henry took me for a tour of the island to all the famed spots that I had only read about. If that wasn't enough he then took me to the cottage where he was meeting the rest of the guys from Rhode Island. There I met Captain Don, Bill, Frank, and Tom Behan, all these guys regularly fished the island with Charlie Dodge. If you know anything about the island you know the name Dodge is synonymous with Block Island fishing lore (Charlie had since moved on to fishing for giants, tuna that is)!

My first night on Block I was sandwiched between Captain Don and Tom Behan. It was there that I was the witness to Tom breaking off a big fish right at his feet and Don catching a 40-pounder after a screaming run. Yikes! He seemed disappointed it wasn't bigger! The next night, after what I had experienced, I wanted to go back to the same spot. Harry went with me, but the rest of the group went to the other side of the island.

When they came down the bluff in the fading light all they saw were these big tails sticking out of the water waving back and forth (grubbing for sand eels on the bottom). They said some of the tails were as big as brooms! As soon as it turned dark the fishing turned on. Even though the biggest fish they caught was only 38 pounds, they broke off numerous fish that they could not stop from going around the one big rock out in front of them. After I heard what had happened I hurried over there and fished the rest of the night, but the fish were long gone. Even though I left the island after having caught only one small fish, I was not disappointed. I had experienced the potential.

It was a year later and I was back and my buddy Rod was with me along with the gang from Rhode Island. Along with the regulars was Jim who was joining us for the first time and Henry's son a real nice young man just out of college. While I couldn't be happier being back on Block, Jim was already complaining about leaving fish on the mainland and that there better be fish here! Oh Well! It takes all kinds.

There was not enough room in the cottage so Rod and I stayed in an efficiency apartment next store. The gang from Rhode Island had been fishing Block for 10 years and had many big fish to their credit the least of which were a 56 ½ and a 58 ½ pounds, actual weight, because these guys didn't mount their fish, they sold them. These fish were taken several years prior on a November full moon, by Tom Behan. Don had countless 50's and Frank and Bill had many fish in the 40's.

A lot of fishermen are not that fond of the full moon, but Tom always booked our trip around the full moon in November. With the size of the fish he had caught it was hard to argue with him. It was the first night of our trip and everyone was raring to go. The good news was that it got dark around 4:30 this time of year so we were fishing before I knew it. The bad news was that it got dark at 4:30 and with only a few small fish around it made for a long night.

To make matters worse for me, toward the end of a cold dark night, completely exhausted, I fell in the rocks and broke two guides off my rod. After a couple hours of sleep the group got together for breakfast and I got to hear Jim complain about the lack of fish. There were a lot of heavy hitters on the island and you just had to go down to the ferry in the morning to see what was being shipped to market to know how the fishing was. No fish shipped that morning.

There is not much to do that time of year on the island with most places closed for the season. With the best fishing at night, it helped to try to get some sleep during the day. After breakfast Rod and I rested for a couple of hours and got up at noon. It was a beautiful day, mild with bright sun and not a breath of wind. Not bad for mid-November, but a little adverse weather might help the fishing. While I worked on repairing my broken guides Rod went next store to get some lunch. I just finished putting 5-minute epoxy on the wraps of my new guides when two guys walked up. They were two fishermen staying in the unit next to us. They were from New York and they fared no better than we had the night before.

They headed into their unit to get some sleep and had just closed the door when Rod rounded the corner of the building shouting, "They're catching big bass and blues down at the jetty by the ferry dock!" This sent my mind racing. Who is catching big bass and blues? It is 1:00 on a sunny afternoon! The jetty by the ferry dock is practically in town! How do you know this? I just glued my rod and I wondered if it could hold up. This is crazy, we fish all night for two small fish and there are big bass and blues during the day?! Rod snapped me out of my daze by yelling, "Grab your stuff and let's go!" I glanced at the door to see if the guys from New York had heard the commotion, they hadn't. I grabbed my rod and waders and we were gone. Rod filled me in on the two minute drive to the jetty.

It turns out that Henry, Frank, and Tom had headed down to the beach by the jetty to put fresh water into their live eel buckets. While standing on the jetty trying to figure the best way to do this they noticed a dark cloud out in the water the size of a football field moving toward them. It took them a few moments to realize that this was a huge school of baitfish that were being pushed into the jetty where it meets the sand beach. Being no strangers to daytime blitzes they raced to the truck for their rods then ran down to the water's edge in their street shoes. They were immediately into fish, catching big blues to 14 pounds plus! The blues were taking the plugs deep in their mouths and not having any pliers they just cut their leaders and tied on another plug. Soon they were running out of plugs so Frank jumped in the truck and raced back to the cottage for some pliers and to tell the rest of us what was happening. Rod got to the cottage just as Frank did.

I figured by the time we got there the word would be out and it would be a madhouse, being in the center of town and all. As we drove up to the jetty nothing looked out of place. As we geared up we noticed there was the oversized "camouflaged beach buggy," one owned by two commercial fishermen from New York that fished out of it. They were passing the time fluke fishing on the inside of the channel. There were birds working off the end of the jetty but with all the bait around there were always birds working there and nobody never paid them much mind.

I walked, not ran to the top of the jetty, first off I didn't want to draw attention and second I was wondering if there really was something going on here. When Rod and I got to the top of the jetty we surveyed the scene in front of us. Holy cow!! There were big blues scattered all over the beach with birds working over big splashes in the water all along the beach and it was just our little group fishing.

I glanced back at the two commercials fluke fishing in the channel and they were oblivious to what was happening on the other side of the jetty. I just shook my head and ran down to the water. Rod and I split up, I ran to the left of the group along the jetty, and he ran to the right along the beach. On my way across the sand I saw a 20-pound bass lying among the bluefish, so there were bass too. I noticed that we were missing some of our group. I yelled to Henry where his son was and he answered that he was out jogging.

Turns out he was out on a five mile run, the last part of which took him along a beach of breaking fish and no one fishing it. Everyone was fishing the night tide hard and sleeping during the day. It was amazing that our little group had these fish all to ourselves. I also notice Jim of all people was also missing, I again yelled to Henry, who was fighting a fish, "Where's Jim?" He motioned with his head to the end of the jetty. When I looked, just coming into view was the outgoing ferry headed to the mainland. Jim decided there were no fish, they were all on the mainland and was headed home after one night of fishing. I was not that fond of Jim but I would not wish this on anyone. Jim would get to the mainland and stop in to see Henry's wife at the shop. She would tell him what was going on and Jim was on the next available ferry back. He would finish the week with us without catching a single fish!

Rod and I were the only ones with waders; everybody else was still in their street clothes, so I waded into the water along the jetty to give myself some room. It was time to make a cast. I was a little afraid that when my plug hit the water I would wake up and this would be all a dream. I reached into my surf bag for a plug. I was geared up for night fishing with mostly needles and Rebels. I only had one surface plug, a big 3-ounce Atom popper; I tied it on and made my first cast. I made two turns of the reel and a fish exploded on my plug and I was fast into what felt like a big blue. I had caught a lot of big bluefish so I knew the feel.

It was the "time" of big blues for me but I had yet to catch a keeper striper. A bass had to be 36 inches to keep at that time. They had been raising the minimum size limit every year to protect the 1982 year class of stripers. My family was used to eating bluefish (I was not catching any bass) so I kept it. Before my next cast I checked my guide, a 14 pound bluefish is always a good test on your equipment, and it was still there. I made my second cast and I was onto a fish right away, if the last fish was 14 this one surly felt like 17 pounds. While all this is going on big bunker, weighing two pounds and up are swimming right up onto the beach. The guys are remarking that they had never in all the time they had fished there, seen big bunker out at Block. I got my blue in and it was definitely bigger than the last. Man can they fight! I prepared to make my third and what would turn out to be my final cast.

It was a beautiful day, and "no" I did not get struck by lightning. My rod held up just fine. There were plenty of fish and it was 2 o'clock and the guys would chase the fish across the ferry landing parking lot to the adjoining beach and catch fish for another two hours until dark.

If my first two bluefish were 14 and 17 pounds respectively then the fish I hooked on my third cast was a 20-pound blue! I had never felt anything like it. The first two runs were intense and I could do nothing but hold on! I gained some line and then the fish took me down the beach toward the other guys. I looked over and Frank, who was also fighting a good fish, was moving toward me. Soon we were fighting our fish shoulder to shoulder when our lines crossed. I ducked down and Frank went over the top of me and he went way up the beach following his fish. It was at that moment the back of my fish broke water! The fin on its back was huge! I now, for the first time realized this was no blue but a big bass! I started yelling and backing up the beach when Rod came running over. Soon the fish was belly up on the water's edge and Rod failed to pick it up on the first try. We were not used to fish this big. I ran down and we pulled it up together. The guys ran over and congratulated me on my first "50." They had caught plenty of big fish so they should know. It sure looked big enough to me. Frank's fish turned out to be a bass of 35 pounds and looked much smaller.

That was it! I was done! Fifty or not I had caught the fish I had only dreamed about. I put down my rod after only three casts and picked up my video camera. With the fish flopping on the sand at my feet I began filming the other guys catching fish. I told Rod to go over along the jetty where I had been, he had his polarized glasses on and he could see big shadows (the size of my fish) swimming in the surf in front of him. The problem was he was fishing a swimmer and the fish wouldn't touch it, they wanted something on top. He was also set up for night fishing so he had no top water plugs, so I cut off my popper and gave it to him. He immediately started catching bluefish.

There were only three bass caught that day. The 20 pounder I saw when I first got on the beach, Frank's 35 and my fish which turned out to be 44 pounds. My fish was a deep (thick) fish, but her stomach was empty. Add a few of those 2-pound bunker and you have a 50. No matter I was completely and utterly satisfied; it was by far the biggest fish I had ever caught and…it was my first keeper.

The guys always ask me if I want some bluefish to take home, and I say sure, and up until now it had never been a problem. After the fish moved up the beach with our guys chasing them, Rod and I began picking up the fish scattered all over the beach. The tally was 15 big bluefish and the three bass, much more fish than we could use. We moved over to the dock and began cleaning them. I wasn't sure what to do with my bass. I wanted my father, back home to see it (he had gotten me into fishing at an early age). But it was our second night on the island, keeping the fish for a week would be a problem. I was not big on a mount, so in the end I took some pictures and cut her up into fillets.

Soon it was dark and the guys came back, with them they brought another 20 big bluefish. We already had too many fish. I am not sure what they were thinking; they got caught up in the frenzy of the blitz. Rod and I kept cleaning fish and the guys ran around to the different fish markets on the island with big black garbage bags full of bluefish fillets. In the end we were lucky enough to give all the bluefish away without wasting any. At one point during the cleaning, I looked at the bluefish and remarked that these were big bluefish. I weighed one and it was 21 pounds, we had already filleted bigger ones.

The school of bunker with the big bass and blues chasing it went around the island and on toward Montauk. For the rest of the week we had little action, just a few small bass. That was Block in those days you hoped for one or two good nights in a week of fishing. The day after the blitz I went back down to the jetty and looked over the water where it all happened. One thing that stuck in my mind and still does to this day is how happy Rod was for me catching that big bass. I have always been pretty competitive about catching big fish and I am not sure I would have been as gracious if the roles had been reversed.

Just then as I stood there reflecting a young guy walked up and said, "There was a big blitz here yesterday afternoon and one guy caught a 44-pound striper!" I looked at him with a big smile and said, "That was me!"

A BETTER PLACE

By DJ Muller

There was nothing wrong with where I was. I was on a good rock, totally content; I was into fish pretty good. Nothing huge and an occasional bluefish, but whatever, life was good because the fish were biting. As I scanned the other side of the point my eye caught sight of a huge flat boulder, I remember it as being the size of an old Volkswagen bus…it called me by name. It was on the other side of the point and it just looked better.

I was on Block Island on a beautiful rock promontory, one of the many you'll find on Block. There was a large cove adjacent to the point to my left and it was dumping hard, ripping right past the rocks creating a long, winding, seaward rip. It spelled one thing for me B-A-S-S! I slid off my perfectly good perch and made my way across the boulder field, 60 yards to what I considered "a better place."

The walk across the shallow reef was tough, I was falling and stumbling, whacking my shins on submersed boulders, I was cussing. Bubble weed wrapped my ankles forcing me to have to pull my legs high in order to keep them free. On this day, the wind had just changed from a northeast to more favorable southwest wind. Yet a fairly good-sized swell rolled in from the southeast cresting and breaking upon the outermost tip of the point then rolling across it. As I got closer to my rock, my dreams grew larger and I thought about the huge bass that was surely waiting, set up in that rip, I couldn't wait to work the rip with my Big Water Pikie.

I finally worked my way to the huge boulder, the walk over was hard and tiring but my excitement won out, I crawled up on the rock, I was right on the edge of the point and the fast-moving waters rushed by me to my left. I stood up straight and proudly assessed the situation. The cove sat over my left shoulder and was supplying a good amount of water and hopefully bait, to my waiting fish. I felt good.

I made my first cast right into the rip and I allowed my lure to sweep. As it did I notice a good sized swell crest just on the seaward side of my point, to my right and rise tall coming toward me. "What is this?" I thought. I braced myself for the unexpected. The wave rolled across the rock only about ankle deep, I thought that it wasn't so bad. I cast my pikie again into the rip about 60 yards out to 10 o'clock; it would swim back to me right in the rip, perfectly placed.

I was in the perfect place…until I saw it again from the corner of my right eye, a sight that all surfcasters dread. A huge chest-high wave rose and headed right for me. It was my own fault for not studying my rock before I mounted it. I anxiously hoped the old adage that God has mercy on widows and fools was true because this fool was about to take a hit. The huge wave that had just rolled in off the Atlantic was gaining speed now and this one wasn't going to be knee-high or friendly.

I did what most cowards would do as the wave reached its menacing peak; I turned and tried to run as the wave crested above and behind me, my lure still swimming the rip. I knew trouble was coming. The huge wave slammed me from behind and knocked my feet out from under me. It knocked me down, I landed on my back and the water carried me across the large flat rock. I was at the mercy of the sea.

As I slid with water rushing over me, a thought entered my mind, if I hit the rip on the far side I was going to be in serious trouble. Drowning wasn't a particular worry for I was in my wetsuit, but a Coast Guard rescue-at-sea was imminent and in all likelihood the loss of my $1000 rod and reel set up plus the plugbag (full of water it was like an anchor and had to go) that was worth another couple hundred. As I skidded further, I immediately recognized the fact that I needed to come up with a backup plan and I needed to do it pretty darn quick!

With my rod still in my grip, (lure still swimming), I quickly rolled over onto my stomach as the water pushed me off the back of the boulder and right into the water just behind the boulder. The hard pull of the water was taking me into the troublesome rip. I did what anyone else would have done I reached out and grabbed for something, lucky for me I got a handful of bubbleweed and I held on for dear life. The remnant of the wave was dragging me right into the rip. My legs dangled straight out behind me in the current. I prayed…hard.

My heart was racing full-tilt and as the wave washed through I finally saw my window as the hard pull rescinded, I stood and raced against the pulling water, away from the rip, seeking safe harbor before the next wave hit me. I used another boulder to shield me as I struggled to get back to the center of the point where it was safe. I finally made it. I did my best to get my lure in, (no easy task). I stumbled and staggered to the shoreline. I sat down breathing like I just ran a 100 yard sprint, my body was tired and weak, I wanted to lie down and kiss mother earth but making out with a rock would be hard to explain.

I sat, collected myself and reflected on my stupidity of not studying my spot before fishing it. I let my emotions rule the roost and it almost cost me. I sat in the warm morning sun, caught my breath and looked for a safer quieter rock. In a short time I went back to work thinking about big bass and what may have been. Maybe God does have mercy on us fools!

THE SEASON OF THE NEEDLE

By Rob Cerny

Every spring I make a selection of a new lure or technique that I want to master during the upcoming season. Last year it was fishing with bucktails. I knew how effective they could be in the hands of the right angler and I put a lot of time into getting the feel for the lure. Not surprising it worked and now I always have a few bucktails in my bag. I have learned that I need to have confidence in the lures that I have in my plug bag, without confidence it's just a hunk of wood or plastic with hooks attached, not a weapon. This past spring I decided it was going to be the year of the needlefish.

The needlefish lure has been responsible for so many bass over the years, only not by me. I never had the confidence needed to fish the lure effectively. I would take a few half hearted casts knowing that the lure was a proven cow killer but some how the needle always made its way back into my bag after barely getting wet. I am a plug junkie and have never been one to pass on the opportunity to stock up, whether I need the plugs or not. Having the addiction, I have acquired a decent arsenal of needles over the past five years or so. I'm a huge fan of Afterhours Custom Plugs, Don Guimelli has a lot of confidence in his lures and in turn it helped me trust the needlefish more as I started the season knowing that I was going to master the lure.

While fishing the Cape Cod Canal one June night there was a lot of surface activity but not many bent rods to go along with them. I knew that pollock were on the menu that evening. The pollock were on the small side, 4 to 6 inches. I pulled a stubby Afterhours needle in a black over gold color scheme from my bag and got a hit on my first cast. The spot I was fishing has a large eddy, and being around the turn of the tide I was able to work the needle at varying depths of the water column.

The most aggressive fish were taking the plug on the surface, these 18- to 24-inch fish were wreaking havoc. Letting the plug sink for a count of 20 or so led to the larger fish. I would engage the reel and give the rod tip a snap, start a slow retrieve, then snap back on the tip every dozen cranks of the reel. I fished the same location for about an hour or so that evening around the slack tide and totaled around 30 bass. As the tide quickened to the west the bite died. Nothing large, the biggest was only about 32 to 34 inches, but my confidence was building now. It was a quantity over quality evening and I am never one to complain about that. Now that I look back on that evening I realize that the first hit on that needle was the most important hit I have received.

Living in central Massachusetts I don't get to fish as much as I would like. Thanks to work, I'm a weekend warrior. I spend a lot of time fishing around Beavertail Light in Jamestown, Rhode Island because I can get there relatively quickly from work. I try to make about a dozen trips a year on Thursdays so I can get a jump on the fish before the weekend assault.

These trips make for a tough Friday at the office, but they are worth it if you ask me. I usually get to the water around 6:00 p.m. and that gives me a few hours of daylight and then a few more in the dark before I rush back home for quick nap. My alarm is never late at 3:30 a.m. and it's back to work for me.

Anyone who has fished Beavertail knows that it is a special place. The crashing of the waves and the rugged terrain isn't for everyone. I have a deep respect for the power of the ocean; it was learned after a close call across the bay on a night with rather unremarkable surf.

As I gear up to fish Beavertail there is a sense of excitement that always builds with every piece of gear that I gather. This night was almost cut short when I buckled my Korkers and the strap broke. The thread had given way and the buckle was laying on the concrete. I was not going to head home without wetting a line but would never considering fishing the "Tail" without the proper gear. I dug a rigging needle out of my glove box and proceeded to sew the buckle back on with 30 pound test Fireline. To this day it is better than new.

I made my way to a familiar rock that produced my personal best a few years ago. The conditions were not ideal for that location but it was familiar and filled with nostalgia. I rarely make a trip to the "Tail" without hitting that rock. I cycled through my plugbag using everything from a Beachmaster Cowboy to a 1-ounce Kastmaster. I managed to scratch out a few schoolies and decided to head around the point and hit an area that had more white water.

The stubby Afterhours needle had not left my bag once since that tide at the Canal. It had earned a spot in my starting lineup. Along with the stubby I had a selection of other Afterhours needles ranging from the stubby up to the big 10-inch floater. Now that the sun was setting I had to reload my plugbag for night. Out came the pencil poppers and polaris poppers and the tins made their way back into their home in my truck too. I loaded my bag with a selection of needles, swimmers and rigged Slug-Go's. I clipped on the stubby and tied a red gill teaser on. It is a combination that I have great confidence in.

I made my way down to the edge of the grass and looked back at my truck to make sure I shut the door and noticed some lightning out over Providence. The weather was far enough off in the distance that I was not very concerned, but the storm stayed in my mind. As I made the climb down about 30 feet or so to the waters edge my sense of awareness grew as it does every time I am drawn to the sounds of the water. This evening the surf was rather subdued. The wind was out of the north, coming from over my head. There was a steady swell coming in, just enough to create the whitewater that the "Tail" is known for.

I found my perch and watched the waves for about 10 minutes before casting. I learned from others the importance of finding a safe location for landing a fish prior to casting. For some reason my anxiety level was elevated that evening. I still don't know what caused it. There is an adrenaline rush that comes with every fishing trip, but something was different about this evening.

I launched the needle and teaser combo past the white water and immediately began my retrieve, slow with a twitch of the rod tip every dozen cranks of the handle. It was still light out enough that I could just make out where my lure was landing. Following my line I could tell that my plug was nearing the edge of the rock shelf, I was in the strike zone. About 5 feet from the rocks I got a hit and reared back, a marginal keeper was pulled out on the first cast. Not a bad start I thought. The following cast I got a double header of smaller fish, it was obvious that the fish were in thick. I made my way to the landing zone and tried to turn on my headlight that worked when I was at my truck, I got a quick flash of red light and it went dark. I managed to release the two fish and looked in my plug bag for replacement batteries. They were corroded, apparently, the Ziploc bag was punctured and they took a swim in the saltwater. I needed to head back to the truck. The feeling of leaving fish for even a few minutes was a miserable one.

I scrambled up the rocks to my truck and had a feeling the evening was going to be one to remember. I decided to swap out rods while I was there. The GSB 1201 (10 foot rod) with 4 inches cut off the tip is a great rod, but when you have to horse fish on the rocks it can get a little over worked. I opted for my GSB 1321L (11 foot rod) with 8 inches cut off the top. That rod became a favorite of mine late last season. I quickly reloaded my headlight with a fresh set of batteries and went over to the shoe boxes that my plugs call home when they are not in the starting line-up. This time I took out all my swimmers and replaced them with every needlefish that I owned. This was going to be a needles only night. I clipped on an 8-inch yellow needle and retied the teaser that just caught a fish for me and headed back down to the water. The lightning was still glowing over Providence, there was a regular glow of the distant lightning interrupted by the occasional jagged bolt. I still felt comfortable enough knowing that the storm was far enough away.

I did the Rhode Island rock scramble down to my perch. I snapped off a cast about 20 yards past the edge of a rock that has held bass on many occasions. As I neared the strike zone my rod doubled over again, this time I knew the fish was a bit better. I was reeling the fish close to shore and I felt another hit, it was a schoolie that couldn't resist the teaser. The pair of fish were about 32 and 18 inches, I released both and took off the teaser. I don't mind catching them two at a time but would rather not have to deal with it when I have to keep my eye on the surf at night on the rocks. I took about

20 more casts with the yellow needle without any more hits so I switched over to a gorgeous pattern called 'rock lobstah.'

Immediately the fish began cooperating again. The bite continued at a steady pace, a fish every 5-10 casts. I kept looking over my shoulder trying to judge the distance of the lightning. It was difficult because of the flash from the lighthouse. I still felt comfortable enough to continue fishing. Eventually the wind increased and the skies opened up with a downpour. The rain was loud and I was having difficulty hearing as the rain pelted my dry top. I decided to pack it in because I wasn't able to decipher the sounds I was hearing. The surf, the fog horn, rain and thunder were all blending together and I couldn't concentrate on fishing anymore. I hooked my plug on my rod and scurried up the rocks.

It only took a minute to gear down and hop into my truck, then I started heading north back to the bridge. As I got to the bridge the lightning increased its intensity and I felt good about leaving a steady pick of fish. No fish is worth taking a bolt of lightning for. As I drove home I was rethinking the events of the evening and the power of the needlefish. I couldn't help but think ahead about my annual trip to Block Island that was coming in October, the island where needles are king. It was going to be a great trip regardless of the fishing, it always is, but this year I had gained confidence in the lure that does nothing…nothing but catch fish that is.

As the trip to Block Island was approaching I made a stop at the Saltwater Edge tackle shop in Middletown, RI and stocked up on a few necessities. I got a few bags of Korker studs, some VMC 3X siwash hooks, and a couple more needles. I also grabbed a couple Super Strike needles in green. A week later I found myself driving off the Block Island ferry and heading to one of the many great fishing spots on Block Island.

My plan for this year's trip was to keep track of how many fish I caught. Unfortunately, after 45 minutes of fishing a bluebird day, I lost count of the fish. If the fishing was that good without a cloud in the sky, how good could it get under the moonless night sky?

I curled up for a power nap which seems to be mandatory once I get to the island. After waking, within a short time I was fishing with a good friend who has been fishing the island for 35 years. He knew where to be at the end of the dropping tide with the particular wind that was increasing that evening. We got into a run of fish that I couldn't believe. Between the two of us we tallied about 30 fish, the smallest was about 15 pounds, the rest were all in the low to mid 20's. After about 45 minutes we each caught a bluefish that were somewhere between 10 and 12 pounds, then the tide slacked and the bite died. The majority of the fish attacked our eels and Slug-Go's hitting at no more than a rod length from shore. At this point I knew that this trip was going to be burned into my memory forever.

We fished that evening until about 1 a.m. and then it was time for another Block Island power nap. I wanted to be at another spot by 4 a.m. I rolled out of bed at 3:30. I would have killed for a Dunkin Donuts coffee but the adrenaline of the bite from the past evening had barely worn off. After a 15 minute drive I parked my truck and proceeded to gear up.

I got to the water's edge and began casting a Super Strike bottle plug in green with a red gill teaser. After just a few casts my rod doubled over with so much force that I was sure I had the fish of a lifetime. I had never felt a hit that was so violent. The fish made a hard run for about 10 seconds and turned broadside. Occasionally, I would feel a headshake and pump of her tail but I could not turn this fish. I finally felt that I was going to turn the fish, it was then that the line went slack and I could feel the plug bouncing along the cobble stone bottom. In hindsight I should not have cupped the spool on my reel while leaning back against the fish. I turned on my light and saw the straightened 5/0, 3X, VMC Siwash hook. I was angry with myself for the way I fought that fish. I asked myself, could it have been my long awaited 50?

Not having a loose hook in my plug bag I took a treble off of another plug and resumed casting with the bottle plug but did not get another hit. I switched over to a green Super Strike needle and proceeded to bail the fish until around 9 a.m. The amount of fish chasing sand eels was incredible. Almost every cast I would get a hit. Sometimes it was a playful tail slap and other times it was a vengeful attack. The smallest fish of the morning outing was around 24 inches with the vast majority being in the 32- to 36-inch class.

I returned to the scene of the straightened hook incident the following morning at the same time. The walk down the narrow muddy trail seemed to go a lot quicker this time. All I thought of since the "incident" was a chance at redeeming myself and landing that fish or one like it. The hit that I received shortly after arriving created an instant case of déjà vu. Another violent hit, the same bulldog fight but this time I was mentally prepared to beat this fish. Yet again the same thing happened and I reeled in my plug with a huge sense of dejection. This time the fish hit the teaser and completely mangled the hook. I knew that the hooks I used for the red gills were a bit on the light side but have landed many fish in the past, including a lot of cod, pollack, haddock, blues and stripers without a problem. The whole scenario was a repeat of yesterday's performance. No more hits on the bottle but the fish once again could not resist the needle and I caught fish non-stop until around 9 a.m.

I became a slave to that particular stretch of beach for the remainder of my stay on the island. I always returned around the same time each morning to intercept the fish. There were no more bent hooks on the trip but more bent rods than I have ever seen.

The last day of my trip had arrived and as usual I played it on the dangerous side and didn't reserve a spot on the ferry home. At about 3 a.m. the wind really started howling, it woke me up in my motel room. Knowing that the weather that NOAA had talked about was arriving, I hurried out to my truck to get in a few more hours of fishing before I went to the ferry to get on stand-by so that I could get off the island before they stopped running boats due to the weather.

I drove to the same spot that I was fishing every morning. The walk down to the water's edge was even more exhilarating that morning. I could hear the surf as soon as I got out of my truck and the growing crescendo of the surf got my blood pumping. As I got to the bottom of the trail I re-checked my gear and tightened the cuffs and neck on my drytop, I knew it was going to be a wet morning. I was walking along the beach towards the same rock pile that I had been fishing and proceeded to fall off a new cliff in the sand. The swell had cut a three foot drop off.

I loaded the rod and cast towards the rock pile that had been red hot and hooked up again on the first cast. From 3:30 a.m. until 6:00 the bite was non-stop. No cows but a continuous bite of 15- to 20-pound fish. I needed to get off the island that day, I couldn't afford to be stuck there for another 3 days, even though there is not another place I would rather be stuck. I left the beach.

As I drove back to the motel I found some birds working. I did see a few birds working the first day I was on the island but then I never saw another bird doing anything more than soaring overhead. Not being able to resist, I quickly grabbed my rod and clipped on a 2 ounce bucktail as the Super Strike needles were having a hard time piercing the wind. I landed a 25-30 pound bass within five minutes and then decided to call it a trip. I wanted to leave the Block on a seriously positive note.

I managed to be the second in line for stand-by and my buddies were in their buggies in front of me and behind me in line. We were the only three to get on the boat that morning.

I got out of my truck and went to meet up with the guys. We swapped stories of the past few days and I got to hear many more stories of the last 35 years of fishing the island. As the ferry closed in on Point Judith we decide that we should hit a spot that should be producing with the wind in our teeth. How could it not be hot with the amount of fish that were still feeding as we left the island just an hour ago?

We geared up again for the last time of the trip but there wasn't much to get excited about this time. We climbed down the rocks and let the green needles fly. I got one decent tail smack close enough to know it was a keeper. There was another fisherman who was getting a steady pick of fish on tins so I clipped one on. Over the next hour I caught a few schoolies in the 14- to 18-inch class. We climbed up the rocks to our trucks and all I could say was "even the schoolies are bigger over there."

I took off my gear and headed north for home. The only good thing about the ride home was the Dunkin Donuts coffee that I held in my raw hands. My thumbs were in tatters from the constant lipping of fish. I looked up to my visor and saw the two straightened hooks and briefly thought of crossing the bridge and heading to Beavertail to throw some needles but passed the exit for the bridge and continued on towards home…more than satisfied.

HE ALMOST GOT IT

By Tony Machado

Growing up my Uncle Manny showed me everything I knew. Through most of my childhood he took me under his wing, picking me up after school to go fishing, he showed me spots from Newport to the Canal. We targeted everything except striped bass. He was a fanatic.

Every once in a while we'd fish with one of his buddies. This one day it was an older guy named Mr. Martins. He didn't work and didn't have a ride but he was always ready to fish. In our eyes this guy knew his stuff and my uncle and I listened when he talked fish. He had been fishing much longer than my uncle had. Both my uncle and Mr. Martins had they're two-piece rods held together neatly with red rubber bands and everything was always organized.

One day we headed down to Sakonnet Point to catch some scup and then fish for bluefish after dark. It was calm, early evening and the wind had died down. At the time the jetty rocks where widely gapped, which meant a lot of stretched steps and zigzagging as you made your way along the top. About a quarter of the way down the jetty we spotted some bubbles on the surface about 30 yards out. Mr. Martins insisted that it was a big fish. So what does he do, he ties on a big snag on. To him going fishing without a snag would be like bringing no hooks at all. Now the bubbles are moving parallel with the jetty moving between the lobster pots at about walking speed. He begins casting past the bubbles and ripping the snag hook back. There's a lot of excitement at first but he doesn't stick anything. After a short while my uncle and I are beginning to doubt that it is a fish at all and if it was, it wasn't snaggable. But the proud Mr. Martins insists it was a big fish and that he was going to snag it!

He lets the snag drop deeper and deeper with each cast. Now we're probably about three-quarters of the way out on the jetty and there are a few people around watching. Suddenly, yup, this diver comes up and breaks the surface. I think I found a gap between the rocks to crawl into to hide my embarrassment. Even though know one got hurt there was a lot of apologizing...and yes the diver did have a flag out.

I don't ever remember fishing with Mr. Martins after that.

YOU CAN'T CATCH IT IF YOU DON'T CAST

By Al Ristori

The key to catching fish in the surf is the same as with all fishing – being at the right place at the right time. As our expertise increases, we do less casual fishing and begin concentrating on those times when the odds are most in our favor. Yet, casting under less-than-ideal conditions may provide a pleasant surprise at times.

I was just getting into serious surfcasting during the 1960's while traveling in New England as Abu Garcia's manufacturer's representative. After getting shut out by a snowy northeaster on Cape Cod that morning I was heading back to Long Island where I lived at the time. My next business stop was in Rhode Island and I planned to try Charlestown Breachway that Halloween night.

At dinner I checked the newspaper for the tides and was happy to see that high tide was coming up shortly. Bait is swept out of the Breachway with the out-flowing current to waiting stripers as anglers take turns casting plugs and jigs across the mouth. I had only fished there a couple of times and just a few schoolies were caught, but I was confident that bass would cooperate under the present conditions.

That was in the days before insulated underwear and I had to put on multiple layers of clothing to stay warm in a very cold, clearing northwester. It was surprising to see only a couple of campers in the parking lot, and I was delighted to see I had the usually crowded jetty to myself. That's when I suddenly remembered that the current there doesn't change until about three hours after high tide. Water pours into the pond as the tide drops until the current change that sets up optimal casting conditions at the mouth.

Waddling out onto the jetty in all that clothing, I hated to think about going back to the motel and taking them off in order to take a nap before trying again. A full moon was shining in a cloudless sky and the wind was howling at my back as I decided to cast a white Junior Atom to the back of the waves rolling in toward the beach on the east side of the jetty.

It was almost as bright as day and to my surprise; a large shape appeared under the surface swimmer. Everything worked in my favor as the bass hooked up and was fought back to the rocks when I realized I had no means of landing it. Not being a jetty fisherman, I never even thought about a gaff as there were always plenty of them among the regulars at the end of the jetty.

Suddenly, a voice came from the rocks below, "I'll gaff your fish." It came from a single angler nestled out of the wind in the rocks while fishing a live eel. Up to that point I never had a clue that there was anyone else on that entire jetty. Not only did the unseen angler gaff that bass, but a half-hour later he did it again. At 32 and 38 pounds they were both better than double the size of any other bass I had taken previously from the shore. And I never would have caught them if I hadn't been wrong about fishing the right place at the right time. Yet, altering my strategy and making those blind casts made it a night I'll never forget. Ironically, after getting up in time to check out the jetty at dawn, I was told that the "sure thing" at the mouth on outgoing current only produced a few schoolies.

MY LADY AND THE LARGEMOUTH

By Mike "Saltheart" White

Back in about 1978 or 1979 I lived in the Worcester, Massachusetts area. I used to go fishing for largemouth bass in Lake Quinsigamond. I use to go way down to one end called Sunset Beach. Sunset Beach has a section where there is a very narrow opening (called the trestle) that runs into an area of the lake which is much shallower and has lots of weeds and structure which made the bass fishing good.

Between the main part of the lake and this other shallow area is a little length of raised ground that reminds me of an old railroad bed which rises to about 6 to 7 feet above the lake level. This rise is high enough so that if you are on one side you can't see over the top to the other side without climbing the hill.

I wanted to go fishing but my girlfriend at the time wanted to do something together so she indicated that she wanted to go fishing too. Great! I only had my Mitchell 301 (I fish lefty) and its matching rod for what I would call good freshwater gear. I did have an old Zebco closed face reel with matching 4-foot plastic pole like they give away to kids at derbies or free with the purchase of a six pack of coke. I figure that my girlfriend will never catch anything so the less-than-professional rod and reel won't make any difference to her.

The rod wouldn't cast at all so I put on a big saltwater lure, a Rebel that was about a foot long with big treble hooks on it that I had for striper fishing. It was heavy and she could at least cast it out and I figured she wasn't going to catch anything anyway so she'd be happy. We fished side by side about half an hour and got nothing so I left her there and went up over the hill to the other side, to fish that part of the pond.

About five minutes later she starts screaming and yelling for help. It scared the hell out of me! I ran up the little rise and just got to the top in time to see her throw the pole in the water and run away towards the car. I very quickly ran for the pole which was being dragged out into the water by something. I didn't make it in time and the rod disappeared under the water.

The next thing I know there is a huge splash in the water and up comes a huge largemouth bass, it must have been around 9-pounds!! It's impaled on the big Rebel's treble hooks and jumping and thrashing trying to get free. It had already pulled the rod in far enough so that I couldn't reach it. The fish kept splashing and jumping clear out of the water. It was very exciting to see!

Using my rod I tried for some time to snag the pole or line or whatever I could to get that fish but eventually it went back down deep and I gave up. Gone was the pole and reel and saltwater Rebel but more importantly, so was the biggest largemouth bass I had ever seen alive.

I went to the car where she was locked in trembling and crying. I asked her why she had thrown the pole in and run away. Apparently she had never caught anything bigger than a sunfish on worms. The bass had hit the plug about two feet from her and splashed water up at her. The surprise hit being so close, all the splashing, and the fish being so big, it had scared the heck out of her so she ran for her life!

THE WAKE-UP CALL

By Mike "Saltheart" White

I thought I'd tell this story about fishing on my boat. It's a sail boat and a damned good one. More than once, the only thing between me and Davey Jones' Locker was this stout boat. But it is a sail boat with all the rigging. Normally if I get a group of people to go sailing, and there is no wind, we troll off the back. I've gotten a million bluefish this way and a few stripers. People love catching fish off the back of the boat.

In 1986, I was lucky enough to live on my boat in Newport, Rhode Island for the season. I slept on the boat about five nights a week. During that time period bluefish were plentiful in the area. They would drift through Newport Harbor coming in at Fort Adams and out under the Goat Island Causeway, then back the other way from the Causeway to Fort Adams. At times there would be several schools in the harbor all at once. Most of the day I was busy sailing or seeing the sights; I just didn't seem to be on the boat ready to fish when they came by during the day.

One night I was fast asleep and was awaken by something bumping my boat. I stuck my head out and looked and saw nothing. Okay, back to bed. A little while later, I heard it again. I figured it was the float above a lobster trap. There was one that would bump the boat sometimes and I would just pick it up and tie it to the front cleat on deck. I knew the lobsterman and he didn't care if I got it out of the water. (I bought lobsters for $2.50 each from him for a long time). So I tied it up and went back to bed. A little while later, the same bumping. Now I was awake and a little aggravated so I got out a light and went looking. Low and behold there were bluefish all over the place chasing bunker. During the chase they were banging into the boat hull. I don't know if the blues were hitting the boat or if it was the bait.

So now I start going like hell to rig up a pole and finally I'm ready but now no fish! I put the pole in the engine well and went back to sleep. A little while later the bumping started again. Now I'm up and hunting bluefish. I grabbed the pole and hooked up immediately. I landed a fish then cast out for more. I was having a ball. Remember though I'm in the middle of Newport Harbor on a moored sail boat. Some fish would get tangled in another mooring line or under another boat and the line would break. Some would go under my boat and surface on the other side. That was a struggle to get the rod to the other side cause all the rigging was in the way and I had to get the line past the big rudder.

Well anyway, now that I knew what the bumping was, I kept a pole all rigged up on deck all the time while at the mooring. I did this almost every night for the whole summer. By the time the season was over, I bet I had gotten 200 fish that way. The pole which started with 7 guides had been reduced to only the tip and one other guide by the end of the season. The rest had all been broken off by hitting the rail or rigging or running boards.

This was one of those things that you could never have experienced without being in the situation of living on the boat and getting that "Wake-Up Call."

A FISHING NIGHT TO REMEMBER

By Gary Soldati

It was a night to remember! A blast from the past. Where cow bass actually ruled the shallows hitting big swimmers like this Big Water Pikie.

Two friends and I decided to head out for a commando night on Block Island on Friday, October 9, 2009. (A "commando run" is where you get onto an island or predetermined area at the end of the day then fish all night and leave in the morning). We heard there was some weather coming in which made it all the better. I worked all day, packed my truck and headed south from where I live. After a 3-hour drive with traffic, I walked on the last ferry at

Point Judith at 7 p.m., after meeting up with my two friends Ted Archibald and Tom White. Being a holiday weekend there were lots of kids and dogs but not many fishermen. When a couple people asked us if we were going for the whole weekend we said, "No, just for the night." To a person, they looked at us funny.

Once on the island we arrived at our destination and got into our wetsuits. It was dark, so we decided to take a few casts close by before making our trek to our special spot. There was not much wind and it seemed pretty calm, not what we had in mind weather-wise, we favor wind and waves. The night started off inauspiciously. No wind and flat calm, these conditions did not do a lot for our confidence. On Tom's second cast he broke off a plug that I had just given him to try out. (Make note of this it will be important later.) It was a medium diving "Slim" in purple pearl. He could see it floating out in the water and asked me if he should swim out and get it. There did not seem to be any fish around so I said, "Go for it!" On his second attempt he got the plug.

At that point Ted came up to us and said he had some hits and caught one small bass. I had heard there were lots of small fish around so I was not surprised. You hate to leave fish but we were looking for something bigger. I had also read a report that had said there were a lot of porgies (scup) along the side of the island that I wanted to fish. So off we went.

We arrived at our spot and spotted the rocks we always fished from. Ted was the first to make the swim out to his rock, he later told me that while swimming, his lure, a giant pikie came off his rod (still attached to his line) and floated 4 feet away from him and a fish hit it! The fish took 2 more swipes at it. He had to hold his rod up and keep the plug out of the water until he got to his rock.

By this time, Tom and I were swimming out to our rock (I have fished this rock since the mid-1980's so, like homesteading, I have a claim to it). I yelled to Ted that if he had found his rock, it would be easier for me to find my rock because mine was underwater. He yelled back that he found fish! I said, "How big?" and he yelled back, "20." I said, "inches?" He said, "no pounds." Needless to say we swam a little faster.

Tom and I climbed onto my rock, a good-sized rock that is easily capable of holding both of us. We got situated, looked at each other and then each made a cast. We both made two turns on the handle of ours reel and we were into fish. We looked at each other with big smiles...that was the beginning of a night of fishing that most surfcasters only dream about.

For the next 2-1/2 hours I did not bring my Pikie back in without a fish attached. At one point, Tom brought his Pikie back in after he lost a screamer and two hooks on his 4/0 VMC treble had been straightened. He asked, "What do I do?" I said, "Bend them back and keep fishing!" He ended up catching more than 50 fish on that medium diving "slim" that he swam out and retrieved earlier.

My first 6 fish were 26, 26, 28, 33, 28, and 36, and we're talking pounds here! And we are only talking six casts! All the fish were weighed on the 60-pound Boga that I drag around with me. We had multiple hookups and at one point Tom had a 31-pounder and I had a 28-pounder to the rock at the same time. It was like a Chinese fire drill weighing each fish, taking a picture, unhooking them and getting them back in the water. After a while we got pretty good at it.

My wife had asked me to bring home a fish for dinner. She doesn't like to eat anything over 30 inches because she finds the meat to be more tender. Oh boy was I was in trouble!!

I will pause here to say that this was not "stupid fishing." The fish would not take a Jointed Eel, and when the other guys used a needlefish they only caught smaller fish and did not get as many hits. The vast majority of the fish came on my new "slim" pikies (8-inches long and weighing 3 ounces), but the bigger fish came on giant pikies (8-inch and 4 ounces) and troller pikies (10-inches and 7-1/2 ounces).

I have been fishing for a long time and I have had many good nights in that time span. There have been nights where we got into a pick of big fish or solid hits of smaller fish but never in my life have I see the numbers of big fish that we saw on that October night. The school stayed with us through the entire tide until daybreak and they were keyed in on big baits—it was amazing!

As a rule you don't walk away from big fish, but we did. We actually swam away exhausted. On my way in I swam over to Ted and asked him how he was doing. He said he had lost all his big pikies and was using a needlefish and not getting as many hits. I cut off the Giant Pikie that I had on my rod and threw it to him and then finished swimming to shore. When I looked back I saw that Ted had followed me and he came up carrying a big fish. He got it on his first cast with the giant pikie and it turned out to be 34 ½ pounds.

There was a young guy fishing to the side of us that night, we invited him over. He had waded out as far as he could and cast with a needlefish for half an hour without a hit. He was in waders and I said, "too bad you don't have a wetsuit." He said he did have one up in his car so I suggested he get it, so he did. We were lying in the rocks resting and we watched him swim out to one of the rocks right in front of us. We jokingly claimed that he kept us awake with his light going on and off constantly, a sign that he was catching fish, and then his camera started flashing, a sign of big fish! So it turned out this kid, Eric caught five fish over 30 pounds while we rested.

We went back out for the last two hours before light and we took a few more fish up to 30 pounds. The tide dropped out, it got light and the fish finally moved off. Between the four of us we had 11 fish over 30 pounds and numerous fish in the high 20's. We packed up and left, back in our regular clothes, with the exception of our long surf rods, we looked like regular tourist. We were soon on the 8:15 a.m. ferry back to Point Judith, smiling all the way home. It truly was a night to remember.

THE CASTING EXPERT

By Mike "Saltheart" White

Back in 1965 when I was 12 years old we moved from Central Falls, Rhode Island to Cumberland, Rhode Island. Our new next door neighbor Ken was a fisherman. I had done some fishing with my father but it was always just, put a worm under a bobber and wait for a fish to bite. My new neighbor used lures. On rare occasion he would come out into the yard and practice casting using a Garcia Mitchell 300 with the matching Garcia Mitchell 2508B rod. He would also talk about catching big largemouth bass. Cumberland has a big reservoir system which feeds water to the Pawtucket area. It was illegal to fish the reservoir but there was a spot close to a main road where people would fish with no problems from the police and he was a town police officer so he didn't have to worry about anyone arresting him for fishing there.

After seeing him casting and hearing about all his big fish, I decided that I had to get in on it. I started saving all my money for a new reel. I saved a little over $14 and went to Ann and Hope Factory Mill Outlet to get the Mitchell 300. It was at that point that I discovered that I was unhappy fishing with a right-handed spinning reel. I had always used my father's conventional and just couldn't get used to cranking with my left hand (still can't). The left handed Mitchell 301 was a special order and went just over $16. So I went back home and a couple weeks later I finally raised enough to get my reel. I went home and put it on the bait casting rod I had. It worked but not good so I set my sights on a new rod just like my neighbors. As my birthday rolled around I still only had a few bucks saved but my father and mother bought me the rod. Now I had a great combo and made up my mind that I was going to be the best caster in history!

I started out casting the width of my yard and then worked my way up so I could cast the length of my yard which was 50 yards (only casting about a half ounce so 150 feet wasn't bad). I then got a kid's small wading pool. About 4 feet in diameter and I started practicing accuracy. I practiced and practiced until I could cast about 99% of the time right into that little pool from anywhere in my yard. I was ready!!

I got together with my neighbor and we went fishing. The spot he took me to was right where Abbot Run comes into the reservoir. Here you might get a stocked trout but it was mostly an excellent bass spot. I had gotten myself a rubber worm with three pink beads and a spinner blade up front. I tied it on and got ready to impress my neighbor with my hard earned casting skills. Well being a kid I was all excited and stood on the edge to cast. I let one fly. The excitement took over and all the practice went down the drain as I cast clear across the water and landed about 30 feet up in a tree. I had overcast by about 30 yards on a 30 yard cast! I felt destroyed! First of all I had made a fool of myself after all the casting practice and second of all my new worm was all tangled in the tree branches and I had only one.

After a few digs from my neighbor like "good thing you practiced so much!" (Boy that hurt), I just had to cut the line and take my lumps. I proceeded to go dig some worms and fish a worm under a bobber as I had always done. I got nothing. He got a couple of bass though which was great and I resolved that next time I would show him that the practice was no waste of time.

About two weeks later I had saved enough for another rubber worm and we went down again. This time I took a couple of practice casts right to the middle, sort of warming up. I then proceeded to work the whole area with exact casts. Every cast was perfect and within a foot of a bush or overhanging tree or weed patch. I caught four bass in about an hour and a half. He had none. I let them all go and just after sunset we went home.

On the ride home he was complimenting me on my catch and asked what I was doing to get the fish. I simply told him that "I was catching because I was casting to where the fish were and it was a good thing I had practiced so much." (Boy that felt good!) I still have that rod and reel after 44 years and it is still a great combo. I put that one up on the wall in my TV room, sort of retired. As my first real rod and reel set up, it still has a warm place in my heart.

THE GHOST OF WATCH HILL

By Andre' Velez

This was the scene of an eerie, strange night in the fog at Watch Hill.

Every part of this story has hints of the supernatural, ghosts and spirits, witches and watchmen with haunting howls and every other scary occurrence you can ever imagine. This story is 100% true.

My buddy Todd and I were on our way to Narragansett to meet up with a couple other surfcasters. We got off to a late start, around 9:00 p.m. We decided to stop at Watch Hill for a quick break from driving and fish for a short while before we moved further east. We arrived at Watch Hill around 11:00 p.m. We pulled into town and the whole place felt eerie right from the start. It felt as if there were others around but the town was completely empty. The fog was overwhelming and the roads and sidewalks felt uneasy. Ghostly! Were we being watched?

We geared up after parking in the lot at the top of the hill and made our way to the beach. At Watch Hill there are a series of waterfront properties, big homes whose backyards face the water. At the end of these yards is a drop off point where a wall drops to the water. Big boulders meet sandy beaches and at high tide the waves crash so hard into this wall that it sounds like thunder. In between these homes there are paths that lead to the water.

We took the wrong path. After hitting the water I looked to the right and saw the lighthouse and started heading toward it. The waves were crashing and so big you could feel the earth move beneath you. The mist coming off the water and the fog looked haunting, it made my skin crawl. It was so dark we couldn't see our hands in front of our faces. My buddy Todd and I both said, "Wow, this is scary!"

We debated on turning around and getting the hell out of there but we decided to move on. As we got further down the path we began to hear noises. We heard voices. It was a woman's voice. We thought for a second it was the wind howling but after getting closer we heard the words "Help me! Help me! Help me!" over and over again. It was a woman's voice crying for help. At this point we both looked at each other and said, "Did you hear that?" We confirmed that we did and decided to keep going. As we got closer the voice got louder. I stopped and shouted, "Who's out there?" Her screams got louder and louder as she heard my voice.

Ghosts? Witches? Demons? Vampires? All these thoughts go through our heads but we decide to continue.

I flash my light towards the crying voice and, "Oh my god!" We looked up and we saw her, there was a woman holding onto a wall for dear life. How did she get there? Was she at one of these homes and went out for a stroll and accidently fell off the ledge? Or was she on a boat and maybe fell overboard or thrown overboard and swam to shore? Or was she some kind of a spirit from the past reliving a tragic accident that happened centuries earlier? All these thoughts immediately went through my head!

As she held onto the ledge I couldn't help but think how terrifying she looked. She was a ghostly, haunting figure with piercing eyes, pale as a ghost covered in blood. She was wearing only a white robe and hanging on to the top of the break wall that was perched on top of a rock, with no shoes or socks on, shivering, crying, and bleeding as waves crashed over her and slamming her into the wall. I shout for her to come down and walk towards me but she doesn't. She continues to wale "Help me! Help me! Please help me!"

Gut check time! She looked like a ghost; a ghost floating in mid air above the mist on the water, haunting, ghastly, like she was in a trance. I didn't know if she was going to kill us or if there were guys around her making her scream. It was the scariest moment I have ever experienced and I had to make a quick decision. We moved closer and I walked toward the terrified figure as waves crashed over our heads and onto the breakwall. With my hand out Todd stopped me and said, "Dre' don't go man!" But it was as if she cast a spell over us and put us in a trance-like state. I walked toward her and Todd picked up a rock to throw, just in case, for protection. I reached up and grabbed her hand not knowing if she was a real person or a ghost or what.

She let's go and falls off the wall, wraps her arms around me, squeezes me as hard as she can, holds on for dear life cries and thanks us over and over again. She *was* a real person! A real person! Or was she? Bloody, wet, cold, white as a ghost and in a state of shock and naked. We guided her to the sandy beach and eventually to my truck where I tossed her some clothes and put the heat on to warm her up.

By this time the only information we can get out of her was that her name was Rose. Rose, a woman from another time? Another place? She had the appearance of a mythical figure from another century, not of a woman from this century or our time. Her skin was pale and her hair was knotty and outdated. Her eyes were beady and her skin was like ice, vampire-like. Her voice was haunting and very creepy. Things were very mysterious.

Now it starts to get really weird. We head for town to get help. By this time it's late. Really late and the shops have all closed long ago. We found a man outside one of the dark shops sweeping the sidewalk. He just appeared out of nowhere. Sweeping the sidewalks at one o'clock in the morning?!! Where did he come from? Was he a ghost? Not thinking how strange it was that a man is sweeping the sidewalk at this hour of the night Todd walks down to the man and asks him to call the police and tells him quickly about the woman we just saved. We were at this point both completely terrified, shaking and trembling.

Seconds after speaking to the creepy man the police arrived. One single police officer. He walks up close to her, flashes the light in her face and asks her name. The woman sees the officer and instantly starts convulsing and crying "I'm sorry, I'm sorry, I'm sorry!" Over and over again she wailed as she rocked herself back and forth, almost as if the officer was a ghost too. She was apologizing to him personally. Then an ambulance came and one single man came out with plain clothes no uniform. He guided her into the back of the ambulance without a word to anyone. The officer and the EMT came across almost as if they were trying to protect something. A secret? A secret society? The supernatural? A group of others?

The officer asked very few questions of us and seemed to want to make this as smooth and as quick as possible. I mean, the woman almost died, was hanging on a wall crying for help for hours upon end. She had blood on her finger tips where she clung to the wall. There is no doubt she would have died if it wasn't for us. We just saved a woman's life! We saved her life!! Not the officer, the EMT, or the mysterious sweeper seemed to care. They packed up there stuff and were gone. Just like that they were all gone.

We looked down to the store fronts and shops for the "sweeper" but he was nowhere to be found. We had saved a woman's life and just like that we were alone again. We looked over at the carrousel and swear we felt something. Were they watching us? Who's there? It was no one.

PART IV

Massachusetts

Another of the great surfcasting destinations, the Cape Cod Canal is loved by many. It was the scene of one of the great blitzes in striper history.

LIGHTS IN THE NIGHT

By Mike DeSimone

It was September 1982 in the town of Eastham on Cape Cod. Art Cestaro was working Coast Guard Beach he was doing quite well for himself. The beach was closed to vehicles so he walked surfside throwing eels. He was by himself and he was hitting some really good fish, fish up into the 40-pound class. He had six or seven fish on the beach and was slowly following the fish south, as they moved he moved with them. *(This was in the day of selling the fish you caught. It was common to throw your fish up onto the beach as you caught them and then you would gather them up on the walk back to your parking spot).*

While battling one fish, something to his left caught his eye. He noticed all these white spots floating around, it was like he was seeing stars, he could not believe it, he wracked his brain and shook his head but for the life of him could not figure out what it was that he was looking at. He thought that perhaps he was having a stroke or maybe aliens had invaded the planet and being that he was alone he was starting to get a little scared. He got the fish he was fighting up, threw it up on the beach and walked further south. Again he was into a fish immediately and again he noticed these lights, they were all over the place moving all around, he just couldn't figure out what the heck was going on.

Suddenly a small boy appeared out of the darkness and he was carrying a very small penlight, he was waving it and shining it all around. Art recognized instantly that he was not going nuts and what he had seen was just a group of kids on the beach all carrying small lights. The kids where part of a project where they brought city kids down to the shore to learn and experience life on the Cape.

Going from not knowing what the heck was going on (questioning his own sanity) to realizing that it was just a bunch of city kids running amok on the beach made him feel a lot better. While fighting his next fish one of the kids says, "Hey mister you got one?" The kids were all ecstatic running in front of him trying to get a glimpse at the fish. Art says, "Yeah I got one now stay back I have a fish coming in!" The kids all went crazy and rallied around him anxious to see the fish. Art was feeling pretty big by now, showing off his "superior ability" to the kids.

Just then one of the little kids says, "Hey mister were those all your fish back there [on the beach]?" Art says proudly, "Yeah they are mine!" Then the kid simply says, "Oh too bad!" And he turns and walks away. So Art fires, "Hey kid, what do you mean?" Another kid standing nearby offers, "We thought they were dying so we put 'em all back into the water." *(Remember this was in the day of commercial fishing, where a 30-pound bass was worth $60).*

Art went frantic, "What are you talking about?!" In desperation he quickly rounded up the kids in his panicked state and told them to shine their lights into the water! He wanted these "good Samaritans" to help him find all of the fish that they had released in the name of good deeds. They scrambled quickly back along the beach searching for his fish. Art was only able to retrieve three or four of the eight he had caught the rest must have had enough life left in them to swim away.

Poor Art, in a short period of time he ran the emotional gauntlet; from hitting good fish to being scared of the lights and wondering what the heck was going on, to the realization that it was only a bunch of inner city kids on a exploratory mission, to the shock of realizing that all of his work had just released back into the sea from which it came. A truly tough night for a guy just trying to earn a couple bucks.

TWO TOUGH BREAKS

By Mike "Saltheart" White

I fished the Rhode Island coast for twenty-plus years but when I took a job in Attleboro, Massachusetts I decided to give the Cape Cod Canal a try. I could go in the morning at 4 a.m. and be at work by 8. I could also get there in about 40 minutes from work so it was convenient to go after work. In addition to the before and after work trips I also started going every Friday night with my friend Smokey.

I did pretty well using an 11-foot Loomis 1266 but over the winter after the first year I got myself a 9-foot rod that was pretty good for 3 to 4 ounces and I fished that rod for 2 or 3 years. I used an Abu BG7000 reel spooled with 50-pound test Cortland Spectron and a leader made of either 60-pound test Ande, green or 50-pound Ande, pink. The Spectron was nice tough stuff and the Ande leaders were also strong. I would buy the ¼ pound spool and it would last a long, long time. I attached the leaders directly to the Spectron using an Albright knot which was then dabbed with a drop of Superglue so it didn't slip. This was a reliable and strong rig that could land any fish even in the strong current barring abrasion from all the junk on the Canal bottom.

One of the big problems you have at the Canal is getting stuck on the bottom or on some old line or lobster trap. With the above described set up, it took all your might to break off if you snagged the bottom. You pointed the rod straight at the line so there was no bend in the rod, wrapped the Spectron a few times around a gloved hand or a hand with the sweatshirt sleeve pulled down over it, and pulled for all you were worth. Sometimes you had to actually walk backwards while pulling. The point is that it was really tough to break off a snag.

Now before giving it the ultimate pull I just described, you would just pull the line straight thru the guides until the drag slipped. If that didn't work you could stick your left index finger into the reel and wrap it around the spool from the bottom and press down with your thumb on your right like you do when thumbing the reel on a cast. This would essentially clamp the spool down and along with the drag prevented the spool from turning. This way you hoped that got your jig loose without having to break the line. So one day I was there and was catching some stripers to about 10 pounds while jigging. I got hung up on the bottom and tried the easier method of clamping my finger around the reel spool and thumb over it and gave it a pull.

Well the reel spool slipped and when this happened, my finger slid around the spool and jammed under one of the horizontal rods that support the frame and this broke the index finger on my left hand between the first and second joints from the tip. Now every striper fisherman knows that a silly thing like a broken finger is not going to make you go home, especially when the fish are biting. So I kept fishing and eventually had nine fish. All these fish I lipped with my left thumb and broken finger with no problem and used my right hand to get the jig hook out. Now something in my brain said I had to get a nice round number of 10 fish before I went home. Eventually I hooked into number ten but it was bigger than I had been getting. It was about 20 pounds. I reeled it in close and grabbed the leader and pulled the fish up to the rock I was standing on.

I reached out and grabbed the fish to lip it with my left hand as usual. Well the broken finger that held the 10-pound fish successfully just folded over on this 20-pound fish and I dropped the fish. The fish went straight down to the rocks below where I was standing and all the weight pulled the leader straight down on my totally vertical rod which was leaning back on my shoulder. The tip broke about 2 feet down and sounded like a gun shot and then a bull whip. The gunshot sound was the rod blank breaking but the bullwhip sound was the sound of the tip snapping like a bow and whipping me across the back like I had been caned like a criminal in Singapore.

So that night ended for me with 10 fish, a broken index finger, a broken rod and a red welt about 18-inches long diagonally across my back that stung for 3 days. So despite the ten fish, this had to go down as a night of "two tough breaks" for me.

STETZKO'S LARGE

By Tony Stetzko

The Century Mark?

It was late-May and I was fishing Morris Island near Monomoy on Cape Cod. It was about 1 o'clock in the morning and it was pouring down rain, foggy—you could see Chatham Light off in the distance. This was before Pleasant Bay sealed up so you had the waters of Nantucket Sound coming in from the south and the Atlantic to the east and there was a lot of bait coming in with the tide, herring, sand eels. This was a noted big fish spot.

I was using a sinking Rebel with a dropper and I had been there a while—caught a couple fish, nothing big, maybe 15 pounds—and then I get this fish on, a big fish! Immediately, she's going … going … going and I'm fighting… fighting… fighting. After about 20 minutes she was in close and she makes this big swirl on the surface, I got a look at the fish and it looked huge, but a lot of fish look huge. Right?

I kept on her, she's running and I'm working her back, the light is going around and around in the distance and finally after another 10 minutes or so, I've got her close. She's there just behind the wash, maybe 25-feet away and I can see her tail and dorsal cutting the surface they were a good foot further apart then my 73. The 73-pounder was 57 inches, I'd put this fish in the 65-inch class, at least.

So now she's real close and she's tired, laying on her side in a foot of water. That's when I got a good look at her and this fish was huge, when I saw her, I didn't move back or try to drag her up—I just stood there like I had buck fever. She rolled in the surf and my line hit a rock with a mussel shell on it and just broke!

I ran down toward her, but she just rolled upright and slowly swam back over the edge. She was gone. I cried…I cried. I couldn't even fish after that (long pause) …but my spirit came back.

The 80

Back in September of 2006, we had been hitting some fish at a spot that we called The Triangle, it was a wedge-shaped bar with several cuts in it near the Gorilla Hole on Nauset. I pulled onto the beach and set up there at the Triangle. It was a bright, full moon night so I snapped on a medium-sized yellow needlefish and started casting.

I was catching a lot of small fish and the conditions were not too good, bright moon, calm seas—the kind of water you don't get big fish in. So I'm there fishing with my boombox blasting on top of my truck, my girlfriend came down for bit. Down the beach a guy I know named Mike was fishing, I walked down to see how he was doing. When I got there he said to me in his big, scruffy voice, "Dude, I had this fish on, man, and it like, opened up my snap and straightened it out and I lost it. It was a big fish!" He left a short while later.

I took it as whatever and kept fishing. By now, the surf was building a bit and there were some nice 3-foot waves rolling in.

Back toward the parking lot was this girl I new and she fished the beach every night too and I knew she was no bullshitter. She said that she had also lost a big fish that night, so now I'm thinking there might be a chance to catch a big fish.

I went back to fishing my little yellow needle—just fishing it slow and steady. When I fish a needle I just reel it slow and steady, I might change the speed a little, but never in the same cast. There seems to be something about a lure that just swims straight in—the bass hate it and they want to kill, it I do that with plugs, eels… everything. Even when I fish a fly at night I do the same thing.

So I'm fishing and I remember, I cast right into the reflection of the moon and I was working that needle real straight and slow. Then I saw this huge boil out there and I felt a "thunk" on my plug. They never seem to slam a needle, unless you're fishing it fast.

At first, this fish didn't even know she was hooked; she was just swimming slowly and all I felt was heavy weight. Then, she finally felt something and she bolted, she took a long run and then started to move in toward shore but at an angle, moving back toward the parking lot.

So she's working in toward the beach and then she pulls a fast one on me, once a fish reaches 30 pounds they are allowed to make this move. She bolted out and then turned quickly and ran in at the beach, if you're not ready for it you may think you've lost the fish. You have to run back, reel in and do whatever it takes to get back tight to the fish.

Then, there it was, a huge boil right in the wash the fish digs in to the deeper water right in the trough and begins to run parallel to the beach. I know she's tired—15 minutes into the fight—I've got her close. So, I get her up in the wash and I get right on top of her and get tight with the line, lay the rod over sideways and attempt to wash her up with the next wave. She wasn't ready.

Down the beach a little more and I'm ready to try again, I get tight to her, lay the rod over and apply pressure as the next swell is rolling in. Suddenly the ring in my first guide pops out, my line hit the metal and just cut it. The fish was just…gone!

I can't even tell you how big this fish was, but she was way bigger than my 73.

I didn't cry after this one, I was just like, "I can't even believe it!"

Surf-Caught 73.833

Nineteen Eighty One was the best year ever on the beaches of Cape Cod. We had so much bait, I will never forget it! It was November and the terns were still sticking around, they usually leave by the middle of October.

I will never forget that night either; I wasn't even going to go fishing. I was just walking outside and feeding the horses—it was one of those real still nights, you could see your breath and it was cold. The fishing had been pretty good; I had taken some codfish and a 30-some-pound bass the night before. So I figured I would just go for a little while. I pulled onto the beach and hit the Triangle where I caught a 12-pound codfish. As the tide dropped a little lower, I decided to take a ride to Pochet Hole.

When I got there, there were four guys there, one of them was my friend Jimmy Costas. The tide was about 2 ½ hours down and the bowls were really working nice. I walked down to the north corner of the bowl and I spotted these monstrous swirls, I was like, "What the hell is that?"

Jimmy came back down from his car with a bobber and huge wad of sea clams and threw that mess out there, I have never seen anything like it! The fish were there but no one was catching anything! So, I had some ranky old eels and this big, black dropper, I decided to try that. I was working the eel and dropper against the current that was working through the bowl, on a cast angled back into the corner I hooked this big fish.

She took three amazing runs out through the gap (the cut) and then back again. But when I finally had her close in this flat water, I could not get that fish out of the water and onto the beach! Finally a little swell rolled in and I was able to float her just enough to get her head and gills onto the sand and then she just sunk in there. I ran down and grabbed the fish and dragged her away from the water.

Jimmy came over and said, "That fish looks like a seal!"

It was later certified as the new world record.

ONCE IN A LIFETIME

By Dave Anderson

As surfmen we are often driven by the successes of others, reading the stories from Nauset Beach in the 1960's and 1980's or about the Block Blitzes later in the 1980's always gets my daydream machine rolling. There is a mystique that follows these casters from those bygone years and I have always envied their ingenuity and the schools of bass they were able to cast into. It was always my hope that I would get to experience something like that and in August and September of 2007 I was lead into a pile of fish like no other I have ever seen.

Upon finding a solid pattern, three buddies had a fishery that could quite possibly only come along, once in a lifetime. Here Dave Anderson hoists a 50-plus inch bass that was released after the photo.

It was in my favor that a couple close friends, Mike "Luds" Ludlow and Josh Clogston had been interested in fishing some of the areas that I fished in Rhode Island and Southeastern Massachusetts. I have never been one to tip my cards too much, but with Mike and Josh, we got along so well that I never worried and we had some really great nights and some real duds—but we always kept each other laughing.

Luds and Josh had been quietly hammering big fish for about five nights straight when I got a call from Mike. I don't remember exactly what he said but it was something to the effect of, "Dude, we have been into fish like crazy, big fish, you need to get your ass up here!" He went on to describe the kind of fishing that I had only read about with multiple fish in the low to mid 40's per night, fever pitch action and an average size of 28 to 33 pounds.

The first night, he told, me they went through two-dozen eels in a matter of a few hours. When they were down to their last eel, and this was a fish every cast, Josh took off running back to the truck to get a plug bag, in the time it took poor Josh to run to the truck and back, Mike bagged five fish on the same eel all in the mid to upper 30-pound range.

A little worried that plugs might not be as effective as eels, Josh tied on a needle and was immediately tight to another good fish. Mike's eel was finally lost and he grabbed a Red Fin and had the same result. The fish were so aggressive and thick that they barely had to move the plug before it was savagely pounded by a member of this massive school of big bass. The next four nights brought the same results without slowing down!

On my way home from work I hit a huge bump in the road and something and my exhaust system let go; my car went from a fairly quiet 1990 Toyota Camry to an Apache helicopter. Since the AC in that car did not work and it was August I had my window down and I could hear the sounds of my defunct exhaust echoing off of every house and fence I passed. I arrived at home and told my girlfriend that I would not be eating dinner, I grabbed some granola bars, gathered my tackle, hopped back in my dragster and headed north.

For the entire ride I was engulfed in a deafening whirr, this meant no radio and that meant more thinking. I was so conflicted! On the one hand I was insanely excited, but on the other I was so sure that it would be over.

We arrived early in the tide and Luds seemed certain that it wouldn't turn on until the tide was just right. We cast our eels without any connection for better than an hour, my enthusiasm was waning fast—when I was jerked out of my glum by a jarring strike, I set up on the fish and a short time later a fat 25-pound bass was at my feet, I was just glad to catch something! Another 30 or so minutes passed without another hit, I was just about to suggest making a move when I heard that unmistakable sound of a Van Staal reel singing under strain. I whipped around and Luds said, "They're here, I had four hits that cast."

Now I must have looked like a guard dog straining at his chain while I waited for Mike to land his fish so I could make my cast (we were in a confined area this night). He finally landed the fish, about 35 pounds and the game was on. As soon as he had a lip on that fish I reared back and fired, my eel landed and I was immediately tight and I mean immediately. Not a giant fish but a fighter, I brought her in quickly—maybe 23 pounds. Mike was ready to fire as soon as I landed her, bam, he was on.

Then I saw the one thing I did not want to see, the silhouettes of three more anglers stumbling along the rocks and coming right toward us! Sure enough they stopped and set up right next to us, just on the other side of a large boulder. My mind was racing now how do I deal with this? We were five fish deep into the beginning of a dream night and now we had to deal with the possibility of having the cover blown off this magic stretch of beach. I looked at Mike and he shrugged—I was sick—I think I even suggested we leave! He said they had been there another night and had taken some good fish too.

I fired a cast, still worried and unsure—and as luck would have it—zzzzzzzzzzzzzzzzzzzz! I was on with a real screamer this time, the fish rounded the point of rocks to the right and swam off right in front of our new friends. "Sounds like they're here again!" One of them said. I worked and worked and finally had the fish coming back to me when I felt an awkward tugging and I knew immediately that someone was over my line. Then my fish made a surge and whoever was over my line set the hook and cut it.

I was livid, I let out a stream of insults and obscenities that would have cleared a construction site. Then Mike suggested it might be better to tone it down a notch as it was obvious the fish were here and that meant no one was leaving. He was right. I made another cast after retying and was immediately on again. After landing a few brutes including one that was a few ounces north of 40 pounds I walked around to the other side of the rock and apologized—these guys were fishermen and they knew the heartache. No hard feelings. I also took the time to try and make sure these guys weren't going to go bragging in the tackle shop. Then it became a really good time as we were all hooking up and admiring each other's fish—what a great time!

By the time the sun was glowing in the east, Luds and I had landed about 12 to 15 fish apiece with probably 70 percent of them weighing better then 30 pounds and five over 40. It was out and out insanity! Now I had to figure out how to get out of work on Monday so we could come back the next night.

The following night Mike couldn't make it so it was Josh and me this time. We arrived right in the sweet spot of the tide this time and after making a few moves down the beach we began taking big fish with abandon. Josh had stuffed an 8-tube bag with as many plugs as possible to see how many different plugs he could break 30 on. There wasn't anything these fish wouldn't take and if you can believe it, this night was better than the one before!

It was funny to watch Josh taking a big fish on a black Hab's needle then a Bigwater giant pikie then a Super Strike Darter and so on. I was sticking to my eels we caught so many fish that night that I actually had to take two extended rests because my arms were on fire and my hands were burning from all the scrapes and raw skin that came from landing so many heavy fish. That night I caught two fish that measured over 50 inches but we had no scale, they were skinny so I'm confident that they didn't break 50, but they were definitely in the 40's. Josh kept a fish that night for a tournament and it weighed 44 pounds the next morning—that wasn't our biggest for the night.

The next day I was dead at work (I couldn't get the day off), I got home at 6:00 a.m., slept until 8:00 and was at work for 9:00. I was dizzy with fatigue but all I could think about were those fish. They let me out early and I was home by 4:30. I should have taken another nap, but I needed to tie new leaders, pack a plug bag and get more eels! When I got home I began thinking about how aggressive the fish were and I wanted to try and see if I could catch one on something totally off the wall. After searching the house for a while I settled on taking the guts out of a Sharpie Marker and then weighting and wiring it like a needlefish.

I arrived a little behind Mike and Josh who were already catching when I got there. I left my surprise lure in the bag and took a spot next to Josh—we were even further to the east on this day (thank God for cell phones, I may never have found them!). We began taking fish like mad again and when the action seemed to be at it's peak, I took out my secret weapon. I clipped it on my spare rod and walked over between Mike and Josh, "What do ya think?" I asked with a grin. Luds and Josh just laughed. I was super-confident that this thing would catch, we had been into a fish every cast for over an hour and they were taking everything we threw at them. That first cast with the Sharpie was my first cast in over an hour without a hit! I made another cast, jigged it, swam it, stopped it, wham! A few minutes later I had a fat 38-pounder at my feet with a Sharpie marker in it's mouth—sounds like a lie but it is the truth, on my life!

That night ended with six confirmed 40's including a 45.6 and one weighing 46 pounds. The tides were getting so close to daylight that we knew were about to lose our grip on these fish. I felt like crying. Mike and Josh had one more night where they started at about 3 a.m. and had fish right into daylight (this was the only time during this blitz that any of us took fish in daylight), they had some real monsters on pencil poppers that morning.

Then we had to wait a week for the tides to come back around to see if lightning might strike twice (we could hope!) I was ruined for that week, I tried to fish close to home but quickly lost interest when I didn't get a hit on my first cast. The next set of tides came around the full moon and we were not confident—I stayed home—they got into big fish again but they were not as thick but the action lasted through the tide cycle again and a few more 40-pounders were caught. The lure of the week was the Afterhours Jointed Eel Mike and Josh told me—a plug I did not have in my arsenal!

Now we were really going on a prayer, a full month had passed since the first big night out there. Josh had to work and I miraculously had the day off. Mike invited me to join him, we went back to where the action began 28 days prior and with a moderate south wind and comfy temps we went to work again. This time the fish were smaller averaging 20 to 26 pounds but we caught a few fish up to 37 pounds mixed in. The pace of the action was no different. We began to hypothesize about how we might connect with some bigger fish. Mike tied on a big 3.5-ounce Hab's needle and fished it deep and slow, he banged a mid-30's bass and then another. I secretly twisted a rubber-core sinker onto my leader and cast into the deepest pocket within range. I jigged the eel along like a rubber worm on a Carolina rig and suddenly, I felt that signature series of short tugs a big bass makes when they take a live eel. I set the hook and the fish peeled off for the safety of the cold Atlantic.

Mike turned to me and said, "That one sounds a little better!" I looked at him and said, "Rubbercore!" He replied with, "Bastard!" After a relatively short but spirited battle Mike lifted my bass onto the rocks, another one in the 44- to 46-pound range. Before I made any more moves I handed Luds a sinker and we proceeded to take a few more good fish. That night I was so beat that I actually fell off of a rock and into a frothing sluiceway between two boulders, boy did that wake me up! Mike told me that Josh had actually made the exact same mistake after a long night there a few weeks prior!

This action lasted through the month of September and into the first few days of October, we just needed to move around within a few miles of shore to find the school. I won't rub it in with more blow-by-blow accounts of the fishing we had for those two-plus months. At the end of the bite, we had all added several 40-pounders to our personal tallies, I shudder to think what the count would have been if we could have been there every night. It was a time I'll never forget and something that truly does happen just once in a lifetime! And I will be forever in debt to my friends Mike and Josh for sharing this amazing experience with me! Thanks guys!

THINGS THAT GO BANG IN THE NIGHT

By Mike "Saltheart" White

My friend Chris and I were fishing out at Smith's Point on Nantucket about the last week in September. Smith's Point might as well be the end of the world! You have to take a ferry just to get on the Island with a vehicle. To go on the beach you have to go all the way to the end of the island (right by Mr. Rogers house, yes, "the" Mr. Rogers) and then drive across the beach to the point.

We went out late one night and decided to stay past the time when everyone else left. I was convinced that if we threw out a swimmer and let it drift along the beach east to west with the strong current, then gave it a twitch right as it rounded the point where the rips started, that we would catch fish. Anyway we were the only vehicle out there except for one other guy who was way down around the point with his truck.

We tried drifting the swimmers into the rip and got a few blues but no stripers so after a while I decide to go take a snooze in the 4X4. As you all know, you sleep pretty good after several hours of surf fishing so I was out like a light in about two seconds. All of a sudden I'm awakened with a loud crash and the vehicle is moving. Half a sleep I figure that a big wave has hit the truck and I'm getting washed out to sea. Not as far fetched as you might think! If you have been there, you may have seen how water banks up like the turn on a racetrack as the currents whip around between Smith's Point and Tuckernut. I'm struggling to get the hell out of the Four-Runner with my heart going a thousand beats per minute. I step out and realize we are still way up on the beach away from the water and I'm going to live.

Then I hear my friend yelling like hell as he's running down the beach towards me using words that begin with the letter "F" and another that starts with "A" and ends with "hole"! I figure he's yelling at me and I'm now still half-asleep trying to figure out what I did. Finally it dawns on me that something else is up. Way out there at the end of the world on the beach, the only other vehicle within miles of us, hit my friends 4X4 on the way out. My friend starts yelling and the guy who hit us starts with the excuses and they're both yelling.

Abruptly my friend goes silent and so does the other guy. I think he thought Chris was going to clobber him. Chris then says, "How many beers have you had tonight?" The other guy puts down his head and answers, "Too many I guess." He then takes out a business card and writes down the name of his insurance company and hands it to my friend. They shake and he leaves. Chris gets in the car and we start heading back. I figure he's going to be calling this other guy all kinds of names but he's relatively silent and obviously thinking seriously. After a while I cautiously ask, "What are you thinking about?" He said he's trying to figure out what to tell his wife because there is no way she's going to believe that we got hit out at the point fishing!

BANG FOR A BUCK

By Mike DeSimone

It was October 1981 on Cape Cod. It has been stated by some as the best year ever for catching striped bass, especially big bass from the surf. There were a lot of big fish taken that year a year perhaps that will never be repeated; it was the year Tony Stetzko got a his first 60 and then shortly there after his the World Record 73 pounder. Long Islander Steve Petri had a 69, Cape local Branny Higgins had a 67, another handful of lesser known 60's, and then countless 50's. Tony Chiarappo had one of his 60's along with many 50's taken that year.

This night was another for the record books as these guys were hitting big stripers at Pochet, heading back towards the Orleans bathing beach. They hid their trucks up in the dunes out of view so as not to be seen by anyone. Stealth was very important as to not give away your spot to the throngs of people that sought the big bass in the day. On this particular night there was a group of about eight guys working the surf and the big bass were active. A hundred trucks rode up and down the beach that night with headlights occasionally blinding the guys casting as well as shining lights on their spot, an action widely frowned upon in surf fishing.

There was a huge swell rolling in that night from the east, perhaps the remnants of an offshore storm. It was a calm night, there was no wind, flat water accompanied this huge ground swell and it was causing huge 10-foot waves to crash upon the beach. This had no impact on the fishing what-so-ever.

As the guys fished away into the evening, the night's silence and concentration was suddenly broken by an unbelievable commotion. A huge 8-point buck comes running out of the dunes and the deer is going berserk! Bucking like a bronco, running crazy all over the place, in between trucks, up and down the beach. The guys were scared to death, yelling and screaming with no place to run, they are pressed against the edge of the water wondering if they would have to jump in to save themselves from this "horny," out-of-control beast.

Suddenly the lunatic buck makes a turn and heads straight into the surf and smacks head-on into one of these huge cresting waves that are breaking on the beach. The wave and the buck collide and the huge deer falls lifeless into the wash, apparently the collision was enough to break the deer's neck and killed it instantly! The next wave then washed the deer up onto the beach.

It was the weirdest night ever for a surfcaster, now instead of guys yelling and screaming in panic, everyone stands in dead silence and disbelief in what they just witnessed.

Well after this these two guys from Orleans, one of them the son of a well known tackle shop owner Mac Reed, immediately recognized an opportunity. As far as they were concerned they had just been handed 200-pounds of venison steaks. So although the fish were "in" and big fish were being taken, these guys opted for the venison, leaving the several 50's and 40's that were caught by those that remained, on the beach that night. They loaded the deer into the back of their truck and off they went to dress it out. Everyone else went back to fishing, like nothing had ever happened.

THE NIGHT OF THE 61

By Al Ristori

Pleasant Bay pro Jim Andrews and I were anchored in a few feet of water on the sand bar off Minister's Point the night of July 25, 1966, casting eels uptide from his 16-foot Starcraft and letting the strong outgoing current sweep them down the shallow channel before being slowly retrieved. Mid-summer isn't the prime time for striper fishing on Cape Cod, but Andrews had caught a number of 20- and-30-pounders at that spot earlier in the week, plus another 44-pound bass.

The night started slowly, though Andrews boated a 24-pounder and lost another. As I was reeling in to get away from his line and try to keep myself awake at 10:50, I saw a huge striper follow my eel over the bar. Fortunately, I was just barely alert enough to push the Ambassadeur 8000 into free spool and drop the eel to her.

She picked the eel up right away and I let her take several yards of 30-pound mono before setting up on the Garcia 2658 conventional casting rod. It took 20 minutes to get the bass back to the boat against that current, and when she came into sight I could feel her belly rubbing on the sand bar as I pulled her toward the boat. Andrews realized it was a trophy bass and instead of the usual gaffing, reached down and lipped her with both hands and struggled mightily to slide my bass of a lifetime over the side.

I'd only recently gotten into serious striper fishing on Cape Cod, but had resolved to wait for a 50-pounder before putting one on the wall. I maintained that resolve even after taking two 48 ½-pounders, one boated from the east end of Cape Cod Canal and the other at Montauk, and was happy about that when I finally realized how big my striper was. We didn't get another hit after that catch, and I couldn't have cared less as all I could dream about was weighing it in the next morning.

The scale at Goose Hummock Shop in Orleans read 61 pounds, and I ended up winning the coastwide Schaefer Club Contest for largest striper from a boat. That bass was 54 inches to the fork of the tail (which was the way we measured in those days) and had a 29 1/2-inch girth. Before the day was out, I was driving down the Cape to deliver the bass to taxidermist Wally Brown, one of the first to do fiberglass mounts that will last forever.

Not only didn't we catch anything after the trophy bass was boated, but return trips the next two nights produced only a few schoolies and no large bass at all.

CRASH

By Alan Cordts

By 1979, I was already addicted to beach fishing for striped bass and by this year and time of my young life, I had already used the excuse of the pursuit of higher education and a profession to emigrate from the Jersey Shore to access the more fertile beaches of Cape Cod. I was a surgical resident in training in Springfield, Massachusetts and I kept an old slant back Jeepster Commando out on the Vineyard, rusting away in a vacant lot, as my beach buggy and my solace. I had access to shelter but that meant asking a favor; therefore, most of the time, I would just live out of the buggy and on the beach.

Late-May, 1979, found me on Island for a coveted nine day and night vacation…an amount of time carefully hoarded from the rigors and time obligations of the residency demands. I was up Island all night bass fishing the big south beaches, rocks, or herring runs. The daytime found me "recuperating," parked out at Wasque Point, and popping for schools of slammer bluefish which would intermittently come in with the tides. In other words, I was fishing around the clock. Oh heaven, to think about this…young, healthy, single, totally unfettered of any obligation for a short vacation time…and the fishing was good!

I fell asleep at the wheel one morning after fishing another long night and rolled my jeep. It is still a miracle in my mind that I wasn't killed. The Jeepster didn't have a rollbar in it, the tin top crushed right down to the steering wheel and the dashboard as the car came to rest upside down. I had removed both the front passenger and the rear seats so I could open the opposite car door and stack two lobster pots in the space. I was probably thrown out of the driver's seat and into this space when the car rolled. Anyhow, I was knocked unconscious. I had a mild crush injury to my left foot which left me limping for the next three months. Also, multiple lacerations sutured, and four broken ribs with a small pneumothorax lung puncture. The late Dr. Russel Hoxie hospitalized me for one overnight observation; however, as a physician myself, I persuaded him to allow me to proceed home for self observation.

The following morning found me out on the beach in Chilmark, sitting as a passenger in my friend, Tommy Taylor's buggy, in some pain, but grateful to be alive, and enjoying a beautiful daybreak and watching my friends fish. The morning fishing was dead, and everybody left. My friend Tom was far down the beach plugging the sloughs; I was sitting there all alone in the buggy when along came a lone seagull which just kept circling around and around in front of me. I waited; I watched and saw nothing, but the gull just wouldn't go away.

I climbed out of the buggy and picked up a spare rod out of the bumper with a big Danny plug on it. I threw a single cast, and the spasms of rib and chest pain that resulted from the motion told me that this was not a good idea at all. I had the plug half way reeled back when the water just exploded. The reflex and automatic reaction of any experienced fisherman so confronted would probably be the same as mine…which was SLAM home the hooks on a big strike. I almost passed out with the pain and I lost my breath.

I caught the fish. It weighed 42 pounds on the hand scale and I asked Tom to slip it back into the water. I am still grateful for all of this: the beaches, the fish, my friend Tom and many like him, and the memories.

BLIND MAN'S BLUFF

By Dave Anderson

Every person reading this book will attest to the fact that if you spend enough time surfcasting, you will make some of the best lifelong friends anyone could ask for. And because you have to reside on the razor's edge of sanity to devote your life to annoying some fish—you will meet some real wackos. It is not all that rare for both of the above descriptions to be found in the same person in our game.

My buddy Don is one of those guys. I met him when I was 22 and he was about 55, the guy just plain loved and still loves to fish. Knowing him has given me hope, because when I see this spry man who is now going on 63 out there giving it his all—I know I too can enjoy fishing for rest of my life. But that's enough of the mushy stuff.

Don is one of the funniest people I have ever met. I have never met anyone who can keep a straight face no matter how far a joke goes—the whole group of us can be keeling over laughing and Don looks like he's doing a crossword puzzle. One day I was fishing in September at Gooseberry Island in Westport, Massachusetts. It was the evening of a beautiful day and the sun was setting behind the mouth of the River to the west. There were probably 50 to 75 people down there, some fishing from the causeway, some watching the sunset, some walking their dogs.

I was at the bottom of the parking lot casting a popper with one of the other local guys named Manny. Don's car had been in the lot for a while and we hadn't seen him yet. There were lots of guys scup fishing to our left and right, lines in the water everywhere. Then I hear Manny (a pretty big practical joker in his own right) say, "Oh boy here he comes."

I wheeled around to see Don staggering down the rocks, using his fishing pole like blind person's cane. He was looking straight ahead—straight faced—and stammering right for us. I did my best to keep my poker face going and acted like I knew this odd man stumbling over the rocks.

When he got to us he quietly whispered, "I'm blind. Okay?" Manny and I, of course said, "Yup!" Don then said, "Act like you're trying to help me."

Now, Don had made quite a ruckus on his way down and the word seemed to be spreading among the fishermen and sight-seers that there was a blind man who was about to go fishing down by the water. I could see them all looking at us, mouths agape, talking into their hands about what was taking place.

I put my gear down and stood behind Don, I took his hands and placed them on the rod, helped him set his feet and got him pointed in the right direction. I looked back quickly to see a fixated crowd—every eye was on Don and me. So I then made a very demonstrative pantomime of what he was going to have to do, grabbing the rod and swinging it toward the ocean in his hands—talking loud enough so that those around us could hear, I described the process and the conditions around us.

Then I backed away and said, "Okay Don, give it a try!" Well in typical "Don" fashion he fired a wobbly cast right down the shoreline and over about 15 people's lines! So, I played my part, "No, no, no Don, that was down the shore," I warned. "Sorry," Don shouted purposely in the wrong direction, "I'm blind!"

I've never seen 15 people who didn't know each other work together better than they did to untangle his line. They encouraged back with shouts of, "It's ok, buddy, no problem!" "We'll take care of it!" "We've got you covered!" I actually started to feel a tinge guilty, but we were in too deep now.

Don reeled in his plug under my close tutelage and readied for another cast, you could feel the hopeful energy gushing down from the crowd all around us, they wanted him to succeed! He fired a beauty this time (Don is a very accomplished caster) the plug splashed down some 80 yards away and he began a rhythmic popping retrieve with his Super Strike little neck popper. No one cheered, but I think they would have if they were sure he wouldn't be embarrassed. After maybe six more casts, I suggested we try another location, Don agreed—but did not break character (as usual).

We turned and faced the parking lot and the people, with my hand on his back he felt his way up the steep incline using his rod again like a cane. Everyone was watching. I helped him over the wooden barricade. I swear, all their heads turned in unison. He walked up to his car, eyes forward looking off into the sky, felt his way along until he found the door latch. Their eyes were widening by the millisecond now. He fumbled with the trunk latch and popped the trunk, I met him at the back of his car and helped him slide the rod through the trunk and up onto the dash. Don felt his way back to the driver's door and sat down in the seat. Jaws were dropping all around us. He started the car, rolled down his window, put his flashers on and backed up. Then, still with that distant look on his face and without a hint of a smile he stuck his hand out the window, as if to feel his way, and slowly began driving through the crowded lot yelling out the window, "Look out, blind guy driving!"

FIRST TRIP WITH MY NEW "WONDER ROD"

By Mike "Saltheart" White

As some people know, I build custom fishing rods. During the winter of 2001 to 2002, I decided to build myself a new rod for jigging the Canal. I had fished the previous season with a 9 foot conventional rod I built on a Loomis 108-30 blank which was a good Canal rod but I'm very tall and decided I wanted a longer rod to get some more casting distance. Since I was building it for me, I chose what I thought was the best blank at the time. I chose a Lamiglas Arra XRA 1205. The blank cost over $200 but I thought it was perfect and I decided to go all out and use Fuji SiC guides. Since I was sticking with my Abu BG7000CL (best conventional reel ever) I had a Fuji graphite trigger seat.

This rod was going to be the "perfect" Canal weapon! I built it somewhat "Concept" style and worked a long time on the exact placement of my smaller than usual guides. As I worked on the layout I was picturing in my mind how this new rod was going to enable me to make mile long casts. I wrapped everything just right and used gold and black thread as I do on all my personal rods. The rod came out beautiful. I even did a double cross wrap on this beautiful instrument that I imagined was going to result in getting big fish every night. As friends stopped by over the winter I would bring it out and show it to everyone like it was a new baby that I was so proud of.

Finally May rolled around and I was headed for the Canal with my new "super rod." I was with a few friends including Ed "Fishpart" Duhaime and Paul "Smokey" Laplante, and it was our first trip of the year so we were all fired up. I parked down the east end and we walked out to the bike path, where it ends in a big circle of asphalt, and turned west to head for our spot. I was walking right along the left side of the path with Pip's Rip below about 20 feet down the steep rip wrap. I noticed something in the water and of course got all excited and was watching for more "fish signs" as we walked along.

Yep, I walked right off the left side of the path and started falling down that killer steep boulder lined slope. My survival instincts kicked in and I was able to throw myself sideways back onto the bike path asphalt but I landed hard right on top of my new "wonder rod." I got up and inspected the guides and none were broken. It was a miracle! Then I looked down and my reel was hanging out of the reel seat. The reel was scratched up a little but its foot had broken right through the side of the rear, reel seat hood. There was a big chunk open on the front and broken on two sides so that the reel could just slide right out the side of the hood or if pulled, the rear foot would pull up the broken flap of the hood and come right out. That damned rod was broken and I hadn't even taken one cast with it! I was suicidal for about five minutes as we proceeded to the spot we were going to fish. I could not believe I had broken this brand new gem of a rod before even wetting a line with it.

I only had the one rod with me and the reel would not stay attached to it.

So I decided to make the best I could out of the situation and found that if I palmed the side plate I could keep the reel in the seat enough to cast. Now you can go fishing in the Canal in that time of May and get skunked easily. But of course, since I had the broken rod, I proceed to hook up into a fish and of course in keeping with my "Good Luck" that night, it was a big fish, like 30 pounds. Immediately the reel gets pulled out of its seat and I have the reel by its crank handle in my right hand and the rod in my left.

After a second I was able to grab the reel body and push it back into the rear broken hood but it wouldn't stay there unless I held it back into the seat. Luckily, I have big hands and could grip over the top of the reel with the line going out between my index and middle fingers and my ring finger and pinky wrapped around the rod on one side and my thumb on the other. The fish is pulling hard and the current is booking so this is like trying to land Moby Dick with my finger tips holding onto the rod. I just kept at it and eventually got the fish in and grabbed the leader and pulled it out of the water.

After that I had learned my lesson and decided to try a field repair on the reel seat. I pulled out my spool of 60 pound test Ande, green (my leader material) and in best rodbuilder fashion started wrapping the 60 pound mono around the reel seat over the broken flap of the rear seat hood just like I was wrapping a guide. I wrapped it good and tight and tightly packed the wraps in together sideways then finished it off with a big square knot on the top of the repair using the front and rear tag ends with maybe two inches left on either side of the knot so I could pull it tight periodically. I fished the reel that way for the rest of the night and got some more fish but nothing big enough to cause any problems compared to the first one. Believe it or not, when I got home, I simply applied some epoxy finish over the mono I had wrapped on the seat that night and let it cure. I cut off the extra length on the two ends forming the knot so it was relatively smooth and I have fished the rod that way, wrapped in 60 pound Ande for 7 years now!

HAPPY TRAILS

By Ken Zwirko

It was Friday, the night of September 17, 1999. The moon phase was just over 50 percent or half moon. Hurricane Floyd, which had become a tropical storm, steamed through Cape Cod the night before and early morning that Friday. I remember that night, leaving just after sunset and arriving at Head of the Meadow beach at dark.

It was black as could be without a breath of wind. I and fellow surfcaster John T. Penschow suited up, grabbed our gear and proceeded to walk north armed with a few-dozen eels. We observed only a single other car in the parking lot. It really was a beautiful night, the lack of wind created a mist that made it especially dark. The large swells created by Floyd were pounding hard on the outer bar as they broke. As we proceeded to walk north we hit a few of the points and bowls casting more on the point and letting the eel sweep into the deep. We did not have a touch as we continued to trek north working the beach.

Out of the dark a figure emerged and as it got closer, we could see that it was a man carrying a huge 40-plus-pound striped bass. He was extremely excited, saying that he threw the eel into the hole and caught the biggest striper he ever caught. He went on to state the same thing happened to him last year on the exact same date! JT and I noticed his tackle immediately, a large white rod, with heavy mono. He also had a three way rig that was all twisted up and still had the eel on it, it was a real mess. We congratulated him as he excitedly hurried back to his vehicle.

We then followed his footprints and ended up in the middle of a bowl off Pilgrim Heights. We baited-up and made our casts. From the second the eel hit the water it was on! One after the other, as fast as you could reel the fish in and cast back out, you were on. These were no small fish either, the majority of the fish were solid 30-plus-pound fish with many larger ones mixed in.

We had a real pile of fish in front of us and there wasn't a soul in sight! That night we each kept one fish, and they were probably the smallest fish. They each weighed in at just under 30 pounds. All of the other fish were released, some were from my chest down, and I'm 6 foot 4! We beat on these fish or should I say rather they beat on us, the entire tide, through the slack, and the turn. We actually ran out of eels, over four-dozen of them. Keep in mind that many of the eels caught multiple fish!

After the final eels were lost we had no choice but to leave. We couldn't believe that we ran out of eels and had to leave what would have been for many a once in a lifetime bite. We grabbed our fish and began our long trek back to the truck dragging some happy trails behind us. It was a night to remember! Who said 1000-pound-plus nights were a thing of the past? After all, this was 1999! We lost count after around 30 fish....each! We kept thinking about the guy who left with the single fish, the poor bastard hadn't had a clue as to what was in front of him....oh, if only he knew!

HUMBLE PIE

By Don Guimelli

It was the third week of June and we were fishing under a new moon. It was my second night on my favorite island, it usually takes me a day or so to settle in and clear my mind. I was there with my buddy Larry Wentworth. We are fortunate because we are able to get out to our favorite island a couple of weeks a year. It was about 7:00 p.m. and we had just finished a light dinner, we were going through the ritual of selecting the plugs that we would use for the evening. We both build plugs and take way too many with us. We were looking forward to a big tide around midnight, with a good moon and complete darkness. I feel the fish are a little braver in the deep dark night. We both slipped into our wetsuits, if you know us you can imagine that sight, and we discussed our strategies for the night.

Larry decided to fish his favorite spot and I decided to fish a small cove encircled with large boulders that also featured a sharp drop. This was a place where I had enjoyed some good success over the years and one bitter failure the September before.

This is what took place…I was throwing a blurple 4-1/2-ounce needlefish. It happened on the very end of a long cast, I let my needle sink and twitched it a couple of times. Bang! A submarine picked it up and headed across the Bay toward another island. I tightened my drag and held on, this slob wasn't fazed by my best efforts to stop her in the slightest. I cupped the spool of my Van Staal 200 in an attempt to slow her down figuring it was my only chance, as the line continued to melt off my spool, then it came, POOF... without warning, the line went slack leaving me to wonder just how big this girl might have been.

With this unfriendly memory still fresh in my mind Larry and I parted ways and I set off for my cove and perhaps a shot at redemption.

Under the cover of darkness I slipped down the path toward the cove. Beautiful conditions with the wind in my face and some nice waves coming in. My strategy was simply to wade out as far as I could and fish the rocky perimeters very thoroughly. I put on a prototype 4.5-ounce black needle and worked the area without a touch. "Sure looks fishy," I remember saying to myself. Yeah, I talk to myself sometimes. I noticed that the water was particularly clean and free of weeds (weeds are the bane of plug fishermen).

I decided to put on my all-time favorite plug, the all black Afterhours Jointed Eel swimmer. I covered the water well, fishing with confidence...nothing at all. It didn't seem right, it was getting on to 11:30 or so and the tides were approaching perfection, the conditions couldn't have been better. I was wondering if maybe Larry had picked the right spot that night, my concentration started slacking.

Then I detected a familiar aroma on the wind, whiff, whiff, ahhh that smell! I know that sweet almost "melony" scent means one thing…FISH! I've always been able to smell stripers, much to the amusement of some of my friends who can't pick up on it. After a few demonstrations I made them true believers.

I got another good, strong whiff and my concentration level went right to DEFCON 1 (the highest alert status for the U.S. military). I tossed that jointed swimmer right at one of the lead boulders on the point and was getting into the feel of the plug's action, when bang, I hooked up! It felt like a real good fish. I'll tell you right here that I don't fish this spot under-gunned. I use an All-Star 1208, VS200, and 50-pound braid. I've horsed in 35-pounders from the Cape Cod Canal with this outfit. I trust it! This fish headed straight into the boulders to my left while I fought to steer her clear. After a few minutes I was gaining the upper hand, yes!

Suddenly she wrapped the line around an underwater boulder, we see-sawed back and forth a bit and I began to get a not-so-good feeling about this fish. I let some slack into the line hoping the fish might swim out of the rocks but no-go. We went back to playing see-saw, and then finally...we had a winner. Unfortunately, the winner wasn't me!

Those darn barnacle-encrusted boulders, they'll get you every time! No problem, I carry a few of those plugs, I know the guy who builds them pretty good (wink, wink).

I was still in DEFCON 1 mode. I put on another jointed swimmer and on the fourth or fifth cast, bang! Another fish on! And it was heavy; the fish picked it up and headed for the deep waters of the bay! Oh no, not again! I was more careful this time and I played her with a bit more respect for her power. When she wanted to take line, I gave it, I figured if I had to use all 400 yards of line—so be it! Remember, I sometimes talk to myself, so I was doing a great job coaching the whole time.

After a legitimate five or six minute battle, (and it seemed like 20), the fish dropped my plug. I was cussing and laughing at the same time, these were big fish I was messing with. I have caught them up to 40 pounds here and these seemed stronger, smarter, and definitely bigger! It was getting near the top of the tide and I started to think about heading to the other side of the island to fish the top of the drop, but that smell made me linger a bit longer.

The adrenalin was still pumping and few casts later my retrieve was interrupted once again by some denizen of the deep. This fish felt much stronger than the other two, or the submarine from last September for that matter. Slow, deliberate, and very strong, I could feel every move this fish made. First to the point boulder on the left and then across the cove to the pile of boulders on the right, this time things seemed to be going my way! I felt a big smile begin to grow on my face, more than half-way in now and she was in the center of the cove and I was feeling good! But this old girl had other plans, she took a turn for the down and dirty!

She headed straight to the bottom and attempted to rub my little jointed soldier off on the rocky bottom. We played on the bottom for a while, boulder to boulder, at one point I was sure I could feel the metal lip grinding on the rocks. Then we found ourselves at a standstill each of us on opposite sides of one of this island's many stones. I could feel her moving around slightly, like she was preparing an escape plan, I rapped on the butt of my rod trying to encourage her to make a move. Sure enough, she moved but she left without my plug, it was stuck fast on the rock.

I pulled the lure off and reeled it in, it was abused big time. Chunks of wood missing, the metal lip was ground and bent and the 4X, 4/0 VMC's were practically pretzeled. At that moment I was feeling pretty humbled but also grateful to share that night with those fish, on their turf and in a place I love with the fish I love. I couldn't ask for much more than that.

I will be back again, same place, same time, and hopefully, next time, with different results!

SO PAINFULLY CLOSE

By Alan Cordts

The incident took place, after the Thanksgiving weekend of 1978. I had to sit out the entire fall season on a cardiac surgery rotation. Nobody was fishing anymore as I called around upon arriving on Island. I drove up to Gay Head after dark and fished what appeared to be barren water, but the tide was wrong; so, I thought I would sleep in the buggy, hidden off the road in the woods, the plan was to restart fishing the same beach around midnight on the high tide.

It was freezing cold, and I was dead tired from my work obligations, the travel, and the final effort of driving the 25 miles up to this barren outpost and beach. I never heard another vehicle, a Volkswagen bus with three young college kids, arrived and parked near me until it was around 4 a.m. when they were finished fishing, packing up and slamming doors. They had nine BIG bass loaded, and they said they caught several smaller and lost several more. I rushed down there. I picked up at least three of their plugs that washed up on the beach, but I never had a hit. That was it for me; this was Sunday morning and I had to clear the Island and be back to the residency. I really gave some thought to playing hooky and calling in sick to try the next night, but I didn't.

I told a couple people about my "find," Steve Amaral had long since quit fishing for the season and was now deer hunting. The same with Bernie Arruda. The third person I talked to was my friend Tommy Taylor. All three of them went up island the following night. Steve quit early and only put two fish on the beach but both of them were 50 pounds. Bernie and Tom stuck it out the entire freezing night, and they were there for the second wave when they put close to 1500 pounds of bass on the beach between the two of them. Tom had one fish that went 61 pounds and he has it mounted in his den. Bernie had two fish over 50, one was 55 as I painfully recall.

Tommy called me up in Springfield the following day. He admonished me to bolt out of my work and get back down to the Island; he would pick me up on the last ferry boat out of Woods Hole. I hung up the phone and dialed up a local weather report for the Cape and Islands. The prediction was for a blasting onshore wind and I didn't go. My friends beat the winter surf to a froth for the next week but never had another hit for that season.

THE SHIP OF FOOLS

By Mike "Saltheart" White

I had fished for stripers many times when I was younger but I was always brought fishing by an older person, such as a relative or neighbor, who knew what he was doing. In 1977 I started chasing stripers on my own. This is how I got hooked on this hobby.

I was working in the Worcester, Massachusetts area on my first job out of college. I had a good friend at work nicknamed Gargo which was short for a long Polish name that ended in ski. We would go out at lunch to try to get a freshwater bass or whatever we could in the "lunch hour." One of those days we started talking about striper fishing down the Cape. His parents had a house in Eastham and he had heard that people were getting $2.00 a pound for stripers. That was good money in 1977 so we started planning on how we were going to get rich catching fish!

The first thing we had to do was get some surf fishing gear. We went to Spag's (famous salvage/retail store in central MA) to gear up. My friend bought a 10-foot rod that he called a "Meat Stick" and I got a combo 8-foot pole with a big Zebco open faced spinning reel. We got some Atom Poppers and metal lip swimmers and a Gibbs swimmer and a few more lures until we ran out of money. We had to wait a few weeks to refill our pockets with money for the trip and then we were off to the Cape.

Our first stop was the Bourne Herring run. The place was so crowded we said the hell with herring and continued on down to Eastham. My friend had supposedly learned a secret that we should fish the high slack tide. We got up at about 4 a.m. and went down to the water. We fished the shore with no luck. Finally we went out on a short jetty and low and behold a school of menhaden came right in next to the rocks. We figured there were stripers chasing them and kept casting into them trying for some action. No luck! We did the same thing that night and the next morning and still nothing. Well, that was it. After a brief brainstorming session we decided that if we were going to get any stripers we needed a boat.

We went to Wellfleet and found a place which rented small boats for the day. It was 20 bucks for the boat, motor, and life preservers. We paid the guy and headed out to the dock. The boat was about 12-feet long. It was a sturdy old wooden boat with what I think was a Seagull motor (little eggbeater outboard). We were very psyched but as we climbed into the boat, reality set in. We had no idea what we were doing! We couldn't even get the motor started.

We went back into the store and told the guy there was something wrong because the motor wouldn't start. The guy came out and helped us and introduced us to a little lever called the choke. Now the guy is having second thoughts about renting us his boat. He starts asking us about whether we had done this before. He was very concerned about our ability to take his boat and return it safely. So we start saying how we knew all about boats and motors but we just didn't know about this particular motor because it was so old. Finally he said, "I only have a boat to risk but you guys are risking your lives!" We told him, we were sure we could handle it and motored off wearing big smiles.

I for one put my life preserver on immediately as we worked a zig-zag (we couldn't even keep it going straight) pattern out of the harbor. The next thing you know we're on the bay with waves to deal with. We were taking every wave on the chin. My friend said we had to go faster so the boat will plane so we rev it up and head straight into the waves. I now know that even with 200-horsepower motor that old heavy boat was not going to plane! With waves crashing over the bow and us getting soaked we made our way to the "Target Ship." The Target Ship was an old boat that the navy actually used for target practice way back when. By the time we got there I felt like I had been on a bucking bronco for two hours. Everything in the boat was wet including our food.

Then it happened, the bluefish showed up and they were all around us. We got our poles ready and started casting to the fish. We had little room in the boat since my friends pole was about as long as the boat. We both hooked up and the battle was on. We would fight the fish and bang our poles together as the fish swam from one side of the boat to the other. As we landed them in the boat we became aware that shoes would have been a good idea (we had left ours in the car so they wouldn't get wet) since it was obvious (even to us fools) that those blues could and would bite our toes off if we gave them the chance.

As often happens we had gotten the cool stuff like a gaff and a fish billy-club but we had no pliers. We beat the blues into submission with the club (we kept all the fish) and managed to get the hooks out without losing our fingers. We fished for hours periodically turning the motor on to chase the school. Fishing in a boat with surf poles can be pretty tiring. We rested every now and then and ate all the wet food. Since we had no leaders we were losing lures like crazy! The fishing ended when all the lures were gone and the blues refused to strike at our jigs which were beer can flip tops dangling from a hook.

Now it was time to head in. It's a funny thing but from a mile out it is very hard to see the entrance to a harbor. We had no charts, no compass, so we came in close to the shore and found our way back by basically following the houses and roads we could see on shore. Although we had gotten no stripers we were very proud of the days fishing. I think back on it now and realize we were lucky that we made it back from that trip alive! That's a day of fishing I'll never forget and the day I got hooked on chasing stripers.

THE LEGEND OF TIM "BIG STICK" WILSON

By Bill Lellis

Tim Wilson was born and raised in the mountains of north central Pennsylvania and currently resides in a small but well-kept home on the banks of Marsh Creek in the town of Asaph, just west of the county seat of Wellsboro near the Pennsylvania Grand Canyon. He is a quiet, unassuming man who enjoys the simple pleasures in life. An accomplished outdoorsman in his own right, hunting deer and turkey in the fall and casting dry flies to native brookies and stocked rainbows in the spring. He taught these skills to his only son Brad, who by fate or chance married my eldest daughter Christine. And that's where our story begins.

I grew up in coastal New York, and being more versed in saltwater fishing than fresh, I started to introduce the boy to some bigger and more challenging sport than hatchery trout. Brad took to surfcasting immediately, and wished to share that experience with his dad, so we met up with my good buddy Luis from Spain and headed on an exploratory trip to Martha's Vineyard. Brad, Tim, and friend Nelson living in the back of Tim's pickup, and me and Luis camping out in my Subaru Forester for a week, which some people find hard to believe with me being 6-foot, 5 and all, but we actually fit fine with room to spare.

We first tried our luck at Lobsterville Beach, where we picked a few small bass and fluke, then headed to Chappaquiddick Island and the famed rip at Wasque Point. The first night was a dark and misty affair with wind against outgoing tide. Nothing was happening at the rip, so I went for a walk and found bass uptide feeding on squid.

The next evening the conditions were the same and I was hoping to get Tim into his first striped bass, so just before sunset I took from him the 6-foot Zebco casting outfit he had brought with him and set him up with an 11-foot Arra, Penn 850, and black Super Strike darter attached to the business end of the stick. After showing him how to hold a rod that must have seemed enormous to him (reel down, one hand in front of the reel), I started a casting lesson by laying the lure in the sand behind him and teaching him a basic catapult cast. On his first attempt the lure landed behind him. The next two about even with his body. The forth almost made the water. I left him to keep practicing while the rest of us set up for the evening. On about the tenth try, Tim's lure finally made the wash and as we were all congratulating him on his progress, he turned with wide eyes and shouted "I got one!"

"Excuse me?"

Sure enough, the Arra took on a familiar bend and the boy was actually into a fish. We couldn't believe it. Tim then turned and boldly proclaimed "It's a big one!" Just as I began to explain that all surf fish feel big at first, the drag started to peel and the fish headed downtide like a torpedo. I'm thinking maybe I forgot to set the drag or something, and everyone started yelling at Tim to follow the fish.

"What?"

"Run!"

"What???"

"RUN!!!"

So Tim took off running down the beach with great commotion and returned a few minutes later dragging a 32-pound bass. Now I'm a noted storyteller, and I make up a lot of stuff when I really get going. Some I know are lies, some I'm not so sure about, and some I'm absolutely convinced are real, but I have witnesses to this event including a law professor who teaches international justice and a noted local female surf guide who helped Tim land and weigh that fish.

So we all settled into a night of fishing and after about 30 minutes Luis comes out of the dark and asks how many fish I have. "Four, how about you?" "Three, but Tim claims he already has fourteen, do we believe him?" "Well, I don't know the guy all that well, but I have yet to hear him lie or exaggerate, and he and Brad are pretty competitive in trout fishing, so I'm guessing he's pretty good at counting fish, but I'll check it out." So I slid over towards Tim to see what he was up to, and not much had changed. His cast landed about three feet behind me in the sand and he slowly and meticulously worked the darter back in, just as I had shown him, but apparently oblivious to the fact it wasn't even in the water.

I moved down the beach, picking a fish here and there. Luis eventually caught up to me with news that Tim was up to about 3 dozen fish with two in the 30-pound range, but Luis was studying him and figured it out. Tim's cast was still terrible, barely making the water, and in a downtide direction at that, but the fish were set up on squid right in the wash and the instant the line came tight, Tim got a hit. So sure enough, we changed our approach to match Tim, which was to make a short cast downtide along the beach, come tight, fish on, set the hook and land it all in one fluid motion. A thing of beauty. Using this technique I walked the beach that night and caught bass on virtually every cast for the entire drop, as did everyone else in our party.

The next night the wind had changed, the fog cleared, and the fish were nowhere to be found. Tim stepped to the waters edge, took five or so casts, and not catching anything declared the fishing was over and ended his short but illustrious surfcasting career right then and there. He had been to the ocean, caught some bass, which really turned out to be no big deal, and was now ready to retire back to the mountains and the land he knew and loved so well.

As we traveled the Vineyard the remaining few days, we stopped and chatted with fisherman all over the island, asking about fishing success, and got the same story everywhere. "Haven't had much luck myself, but I hear some guy from Pennsylvania caught a pair of 30's over at Wasque the other night." So I made up a fake wanted poster with Tim's picture on it that proclaimed: "WANTED for FISH MURDER" TIM WILSON aka TIM "BIG STICK" WILSON, aka "PENNSYLVANIA TIM, aka "some guy from PENNSYLVANIA", which now proudly hangs on the wall of a garage along the banks of Marsh Creek in the town of Asaph in the mountains of north central Pennsylvania. And after a hard day of deer hunting, the local boys gather round the wood stove, pound a few beers, and retell the tale that will surely be passed down from generation to generation to come, of the Legend of Tim "Big Stick" Wilson.

SHOULD I STAY OR SHOULD I GO?

By Dave Anderson

It was a good day to be a bass fisherman! Stripers went crazy on mackerel, herring, and other baitfish, all those on hand had an experience that may never be repeated.

The period of time from May 20 to June 20 is an amazing time to be on the water in New England and when I asked my buddy DJ Muller to come up and fish the upside of the new moon in June 2008 he was more than happy to team up with me along some of the tidal rivers in southeastern Massachusetts. We had two great nights of fishing with loaded Red Fins, taking several quality fish into the low-20-pound range. We had a blast.

It was DJ's last morning in town that has left me firmly planted under the heel of his boot for the last three years. We elected to go and try the Cape Cod Canal even though the tide was a little earlier than what I would have hoped for. Sure enough, the water was screaming east and fishing was tough.

We tried and found almost nothing, I had one half-hearted hit on a pencil and that was it. Tired from two-plus days with little sleep, we headed for the house. On the way back I realized that my cell phone was not in my pocket and flipped open the glove box in my car to find that I had three missed calls—all from the hours we were at the Canal and all from my friend Casey. We were already almost all the way home when I called him back to find out that the east end of the Canal had been hot all morning. Casey had taken several good fish including a few in the 30's and one at 35-pounds—all on topwater plugs.

I can't write what DJ had to say in response to this but he was due back in Jersey the next day, poor bastard—I, on the other hand, had another date with the Canal.

Casey said that there were medium-sized mackerel in the Canal and that the East End was alive with bait. Seemed like a logical stop for the next day. I arrived with my bag packed with care, my boots were on the sand at Pip's Rip long before the sun and I began casting a large swimmer while waiting for first light.

It was a cloudy and cold day with northeast winds so there was no real sunrise, just that whitish glow that pushes through the cloud-cover. Suddenly it was light and everything was right—it would happen any minute. Forty-five minutes later and the big moment had still not come and now there were hundreds of people standing with their rods and not casting.

This was one of those times when I had to make that fateful decision; should I stay or should I go. I always dread making that decision because I have left just before the mayhem a few times and it haunts me for months when I do. After about 14 "last casts" I finally headed for the vehicle. I was so disgusted with myself for chasing a day-old report that I was berating myself out loud in the car.

"Why, did I listen to him!?" "These things never pan out and I should know better!" "Now I'm going to be useless at the office and I've made my 70 minute commute into a 110 minute commute!" On and on I went and then from high on the hill just east of the herring run I looked into the Canal and saw a single fish break. I figured I should at least take a cast, after all I was already there.

Upon entering the parking lot, I was having trouble finding a spot—something wasn't adding up and adrenalin began trickling into my veins. I pulled off to the left in the lot, grabbed my gear and ran down the cement steps to the water. People were spaced evenly along the entire stretch from the Cribbin to Muscle Bed, a distance of more than a mile. I knew a spot with steep, weedy rocks where no one would stand and found it just big enough to fit into without bothering my neighbors.

Looking left and then right, not one rod was bent. Focusing further I could see white bellies gleaming in the dull overcast light. "I must have just missed them," I thought. Then a guy three spots down was tight to something that looked decent. I snapped on a bunker-colored pencil and fired a long cast, I worked the plug three feet and it was viciously assaulted. My rod doubled and in short order I had a 46-inch bass laying at my feet. I reached back for my pliers and realized that in my haste to get down to the water I had not put my belt back on! I carefully removed the hooks manually and released the bass that I would estimate to weigh around 35 pounds.

I quickly launched another long shot, worked the plug a few feet, slam! Fish on again, this one weighing around 25, another cast another fish in the upper 20's. Then all hell broke loose. About 50 yards out and just upcurrent, the water erupted. You could see a defined line of bass pushing waves of leaping mackerel downtide. The pops were loud and the lightning-quick bursts of white water each marked the death of another mack. I couldn't get my line off the roller fast enough, I bet I looked like it was my first day fishing as I tried to manage a cast amid all the mayhem. I got my plug out there and got nothing in return, then another cast with nothing. Maybe too much bait?

Then I heard a voice to my left shout "holy shit, look at that!"

A small pod of adult bunker was racing along the shore, not 15 feet away from the rocks and huge torpedo-like swells were following closely behind them. They swam right by me and let me tell you those fish were giants. I watched as about 60 plugs landed on them—not one was taken. Schools of terrified macks would come in along the rocks every few minutes—looking down the shore in either direction now revealed dozens of doubled rods, thrashing fish and flying plugs—it looked like Normandy!

The water in front of me had fallen quiet and I went back to blind casting. The action was back on in a big way. It was stupid, you could catch all the 20's you wanted—but I wanted one of those giants. It was at about this time that a young kid skidded down the rocks next to me and began casting a tiny popper. He wasn't hooking up at all while everyone around him was.

I turned to him and asked if he had any bigger plugs. He said he didn't and I could see the desperation growing in his eyes. I opened my bag and handed him a brand new Guppy pencil popper. "No!" he said, "I don't want to take your plug!" I looked at him sternly and said, "Listen, I want to catch another fish and I'm not going to argue with you, take the plug and catch a fish for crissakes!"

He tried to convey his thanks but I was already busy working my pencil again. On this cast I didn't get a hit until the plug was halfway in. The plug was violently popped three-feet out of the water three times—the fish kept missing! Staying calm, I held the plug on a tight line in the current and rocked it slowly so it just teetered in one place. There was no fantastic explosion this time, just a light pop and a toilet-flush swirl—my plug disappeared. The kid walked away to give me some room and the battle was on.

After setting the hook I quickly determined that this fish was a different animal, she was peeling downtide with very little effort it became clear that my drag setting was no match for this fish. I put more pressure on her by raising my rod tip and leaning into her weight. A few times I brought her to the surface where she would throw a massive spray of white water as she defiantly dove for deeper water. Each time she came up casts would arc in from every direction. I tried to call down the shore to these people but it was clear that these were real rookies tossing 4-ounce plugs with trout rods who had been alerted by cell phone—they weren't even hearing me. They saw my fish as their chance to hook up, this was not looking good.

After the third time I brought her to the surface and received the subsequent volley of plugs from the googan gallery I decided that I had to take drastic action or risk becoming entangled with 400 lines, losing the fish and perhaps earning an aggravated assault charge in the process. I grabbed the spool and gingerly attempted to turn the fish. As the spool slipped in fits under my fingers, there was a pivotal moment when I could tell that everything was pushed to the max, I waited for something to break, my rod perhaps, but she turned! I had her head now! I worked her back several yards while she shook her head violently in protest. Apparently she was just taking a rest though, because she suddenly turned and bolted, my rod bucked once and my line fell slack. I reeled in to find two hooks on the front treble straight as pins and one on the rear treble bent half-open.

I was sick—but just for a minute as there were fish breaking everywhere and I was sure I would have another chance. Well, that chance did not come. I caught several more good fish and followed the schools east with the tide—but nothing over 30 pounds. I returned to the herring run lot at about 11:30 a.m. and found my friend Ryan Smith the plug builder and a few friends straddling their bikes. They had stories just like mine and they had bested a few fish that went a bit north of the 40-pound mark. My friend Paul Moriarty showed next with a story of a guy fishing a schoolie rig with 15-pound mono that he helped land a fish in the mid-40's caught on an old blue/white Atom Popper.

Suddenly, while talking to Ryan I saw huge breaks blasting down by the Sagamore Bridge. I looked at everyone around me and they said they were too tired to chase again. I ran down there alone only to find the fish were out of range. As they moved with the current, they came very close to the other shore and a man burst out of the trees and flipped a short cast into the melee. It took all of five seconds to see and hear his plug go down. To this day, those are still the largest splashes I've seen feeding stripers make!

I began blind casting while I watched this guy battling his big fish at peak current when my chartreuse/white pencil was blasted. I fought this heavy fish for a bit, it wrapped me on a lobster pot, I moved around and finally freed it. I got the fish in and weighed it, 33 pounds—I looked across the ditch and this guy was still on the same fish! Now another angler was waiting at his side. After a long battle, the fish was thrashing in close and his buddy waded in and grabbed it. I was over 600-feet away and I could see this fish was a beast. There were still some huge breaks exploding all around, but when he finally got that fish in his hands he let out a Tarzan-like scream and carried it right up to the car and left—even with huge breaks all around him. I never saw that fish up close—but it had to be huge to pull him away from that kind of action.

After a few more fish, the blitz was over and I headed back to the lot with my camera to capture the carnage. There were big, dead bass and happy anglers everywhere. I saw quite a few 40's that day, I called Red Top later and they couldn't even sum up the days weigh-ins. There had been so many big fish that none of them seemed more significant that the next. It was truly one of those days that I'll never forget—but I would give it all up just to see the one I lost.

I ran into the kid again a few days later and he was all smiles—after losing a few fish he caught some good fish up to 27 pounds on the Guppy before a rolling bass cut his leader. In some weird way, that was more satisfying than all of the fish I caught or lost during the blitz—and besides you gotta love a kid who borrows his dad's car to skip school and go fishing!